Why Grow That When You Can Grow This?

WHY GROW THAT WHEN YOU CAN GROW THIS?

255 Extraordinary Alternatives to Everyday Problem Plants

ANDREW KEYS

Timber Press
Portland | London

Book design by
Kate Giambrone & Julianna Johnson

Published in 2012 by Timber Press, Inc.

The Haseltine Building
133 S.W. Second Avenue, Suite 450
Portland, Oregon 97204-3527
timberpress.com

2 The Quadrant
135 Salusbury Road
London NW6 6RJ
timberpress.co.uk

Printed in China

Library of Congress Cataloging-in-Publication Data
Keys, Andrew.
        Why grow that when you can grow this? : 255
extraordinary alternatives to everyday problem plants /
Andrew Keys. -- 1st ed.
        p. cm.
   Includes bibliographical references and index.
   ISBN 978-1-60469-286-0
  1. Low maintenance gardening. 2. Vegetation and
climate. I. Title.
   SB473.K535 2012
   581.7'22--dc23

                                    2012003943

A catalog record for this book is also
available from the British Library.

For BK

8 Preface

10 Acknowledgments

Upgrade Your Garden

15 Forbidden Fruit

19 How to Choose All-Star Plants

Everyday Problem Plants and Extraordinary Alternatives

35

TREES
Banana 36, Bay 39, Birch 42, Blue spruce 46, Callery pear 49, Citrus 52, Dogwood 56, Elm 59, Hemlock 62, Italian cypress 65, Jacaranda 68, Japanese maple 72, Live oak 75, Lombardy poplar 78, Magnolia 81, Mimosa 84, Norway maple 87, Olive 90, Ornamental fruit trees 94, Weeping willow 97

101

SHRUBS
Arborvitae 102, Barberry 105, Boxwood 108, Burning bush 112, Camellia 116, Crape myrtle 119, Daphne 122, Dwarf rhododendron 125, Forsythia 128, Harry Lauder's walking stick 131, Holly 134, Hydrangea 138, Juniper 141, Lilac 144, Palm 147, Pieris 150, Privet 154, Pussy willow 157, Pyracantha 160, Rhododendron 164, Rose—hybrid tea 167, Scotch broom 170, Spirea 173, Yew 176

Resources

320 Recommended Reading

321 Web Sites with More Information

Contents

181

VINES

Asian bittersweet 182, Clematis—large-flowered 185, Climbing rose 188, English ivy 191, Japanese honeysuckle 194, Wisteria 197

201

PERENNIALS

Agave 202, Astilbe 205, Baby's breath 208, Bleeding heart 211, Canna 214, Chrysanthemum 218, Daylily 222, Delphinium 225, Dusty miller 228, Fern 231, Forget-me-not 234, Foxglove 238, Gladiolus 241, Goldenrod 244, Hosta 248, Iris—bearded 251, Lavender 254, Peony 257, Phlox 260, Poppy 264, Prickly pear 267, Primrose 270, Yucca 274

279

GRASSES AND GROUNDCOVERS

Bamboo 280, Bishop's weed 283, Creeping juniper 286, Dwarf fountain grass 290, Lawn grass 294, Lily of the valley 297, Miscanthus 300, Moss 303, Pachysandra 306, Pampas grass 309, Vinca 312, Wintercreeper 315

322

Mail-Order Sources for Plants

325

Metric Conversions

326

Photography Credits

328

Index

336

About the Author

Preface

It's a tired turn of phrase, but the grass is always greener on the other side—really, it is. As human beings in general, and gardeners especially, why do we always covet what we can't have?

I was born and raised in the Deep South, land of soaring magnolias, stifling humidity, red clay, and winters that did not require a heavy coat. Life was muggy. I remember sixty-degree Christmases.

Early on, I came to love a certain brand of pushy, jungly, subtropical plants, the likes of which hung out in the woods behind my childhood home. Those plants were the characters that populated the best playground ever for a kid with an interest in nature, and they make up a big chunk of my concept of the place. It was lush—almost tropical, but not quite.

Everything changed when my interest in plants took on more dimension, and when I discovered plants of the arid landscape. Overnight, my affections turned from my native flora to all plants low-water, especially those silvery, wispy plants found in Mediterranean climates—they were too cool for school. An interview I read of a lavender farmer in Big Sur, California, set in motion a lifelong fixation that, at the time, was more than a tad laughable. Sure, drought happens in the South, but if there's one thing Mississippi is not, it's arid.

Years later, I moved to New England. Humidity here isn't nearly the beast it is in the South, and while Boston definitely isn't arid, I found I could grow a few of those Mediterranean plants I had so wished for growing up. The irony was I found myself pining for those jungly southern plants I took for granted growing up there.

I tried nurturing maybe-hardy dwarf palmetto *(Sabal minor)* through the long New England winter, and struggled to grow angel trumpet *(Brugmansia)* in the fleeting summer. None of them made it. Partly, they were victims of Mother Nature, and partly my own pragmatism: I do not have the patience to baby a plant. I try a lot of plants, and if one doesn't grow, that's that. I use compost for fertilizer, and I'll rip out a bug-prone plant before I spray it with poisonous chemicals. I live in a climate where I think plants should never need extra water after they're settled in. Those plants I wished I could grow required unsustainable measures of all kinds, not to mention more heartache than one should ever have over a plant (which is to say, none). I didn't give up completely, but I started looking for alternatives.

For some reason, I'm captivated by plants that manage to look and feel like other plants. The idea that evolution could spit out two similar plants with similar flowers on opposite sides of the globe—that, to me, is mind-blowing. In my desire to evoke the look and feel of plants I couldn't grow, I found myself turning to these kinds of plants—similar, but more sustainable in my garden.

What I hadn't realized was how powerful plants can be in channeling long ago, faraway places I'd lived or visited, how plants can transport us, the sentimentality they can trigger. To me, plants are as much a window into another time as a high school yearbook. But high school is over, and there's no sense in trying to relive it when you've moved on to better things. I realized there's no reason to struggle to grow a plant I simply can't, not when the plant kingdom is chock full of gems for every climate and situation, plants that are the same in so many ways as whatever weed you're wishing for.

Follow me as I show you how to find them. It'll require a little patience, a tiny bit of sacrifice, and some out-of-the-box thinking, but really, it's simple. In the end, you'll be rewarded with the means to choose plants that are better and more sustainable for you and your garden in every way.

Acknowledgments

So many people helped put this book together. Thanks to confidants and co-conspirators Brian Katzen, Amanda Thomsen, Pamela Price, Bob, Victoria Harres, Michelle and Michael Forman, Susan Morrison, and Lynn Felici-Gallant. Thanks to Ivette Soler, Debra Lee Baldwin, Margaret Roach, Amy Stewart, and Steve Aitken for sharing a wealth of knowledge and supporting me as a new author. Thanks to Timber Press for believing in the idea.

Thanks to Michelle Gervais at *Fine Gardening* for being both a friend and the first to say, "Hey, would you be interested in contributing an article?" before I'd ever thought of writing a book. Thanks to Rebecca Sweet for amazing advice and hospitality, and the best pep talk ever.

Thanks to my family, especially my parents, who told me to go play in the woods instead of playing video games.

Thanks to the incredible community of friends I've made in the gardening world through social media. This book wouldn't have happened without you.

Thanks to my colleagues at my job outside the world of plants at the Isabella Stewart Gardner Museum in Boston for your patience on days when the book demanded more attention.

Thanks to all the arboreta, botanic gardens, nurseries, and private homeowners who grow beautiful plants, many of which appear in photos in these pages: the Arnold Arboretum of Harvard University; Jill Nooney, Bob Munger, and Bedrock Gardens; Van Berkum Nursery; Millican Nurseries; Long Hill and Sedgwick Gardens; Kristin Green and Blithewold Mansion, Gardens, and Arboretum; Tower Hill Botanic Garden; New York Botanical Garden; City of Boston Parks and Recreation; Mindy Arbo, Dudley Cotton, and the Cotton-Arbo retum; Stonepost Nursery; John Gallant and Katsura Gardens; Kathy Tracey and Avant Gardens; Stonecrop Gardens; the Arboretum at the University of California, Santa Cruz; Elayne Takemoto, Claire Woods, Kelly Kilpatrick, Megan Speckmann, and Annie's Annuals; Andy Brand, Chris Koppel, and Broken Arrow Nursery; Martha Morrison; Jody Clineff; Fort Worth Botanical Gardens; San Francisco Botanical Garden; the Guido family, who also made cookies.

Upgrade Your Garden

Creeping sedum (*Sedum*) excels in dry places moss can't, and lamb's ear (*Stachys byzantina*) looks better than dusty miller (*Senecio cineraria*) year after year.

Flowers of mountain laurel (*Kalmia latifolia*) beat
dwarf rhododendron by a mile.

Forbidden Fruit

Let's face it: the garden is a popularity contest.
High school is a metaphor for life, and gardening is no
exception. Step into our gardens and we find the prom
queen and the star quarterback, the cheerleader and
the rebel who cut class. Popular plants rule today's
landscapes the same way popular kids rule the school.
But just like kids, plants grow up, and ten years or
two growing seasons later, we wonder, "Why did my
homecoming queen, that gorgeous hybrid tea rose I
planted, grow into such a mess?"

In truth, we're as sentimental about fashionable plants as we are for that sophomore summer we dated the class rebel. So many of our garden favorites aren't just plants we've grown up with—plants our mothers grew in some distant garden long ago, in an ideal climate—they're also plants *gardening* grew up with as a tradition in itself. These plants came to popularity in Victorian England, the cradle of garden humanity, its climate ideal for many and very different from most of North America.

The difference between high school and gardening is this: while the homecoming queen may have lost her luster by the ten-year reunion, we're just as likely to open a glossy garden mag to a luscious spread of roses today as we were a hundred years ago. We are sentimental, and our attachment to well-liked plants is truly the stuff of high school legend that too often ends in heartache.

But what if we could harness that sentimentality for good? Plenty of the less popular kids in school—the kids from the A/V club and the softball team, the show choir and the band geeks—turned out to be stars. What if there were problem-solvers in the plant world that grew into fabulous, successful, garden-worthy citizens in spite of not having started out as trendy plants?

The good news is, there are.

In recent years we have slowly come to realize this. Low-care grasses have come up in popularity, as have low-water plants for dry climates and native plants of all kinds. We are savvier about growing plants that will succeed in their site and climate. The missing link in bringing the "right plant, right place" philosophy to the mainstream is to connect these plant problem-solvers to our sentimental attachment to best-loved plants.

Acting Out

Why do so many popular plants grow up to be garden rejects?

To answer this, we must first abandon the idea of plants as yard furniture and remember that, like the students in our high school metaphor, plants are living things. Like people, plants come with baggage.

All plants have origins, even varieties bred by people. The parents of every plant at the local nursery adapted to grow within the parameters of a certain niche in a specific place. When we replicate those conditions in our gardens, we allow plants to grow into good citizens, both culturally and aesthetically.

Culturally means the plant thrives because its basic needs are met, such as the high and low temperatures it prefers and type of soil. *Aesthetically* means the plant brings its full sensory potential to the table—yes, especially how it looks, but also how it smells, feels, tastes, and even how it sounds.

Depending on the plant and the place, providing for plants can be a snap, or it can be impossible. Plants usually act out when we can't give them what they need to succeed. That's when popular plants mature into problem children.

Let's be honest. If we've picked up this book, we've probably:

- Pampered the one-time prom king in a pot indoors, because he'd be a plantsicle outside in winter
- Fed the aging drama queen's chemical habit, lest she be overrun by bugs and slugs
- Sneaked out at night to water the thirsty freeloader who wilted during a watering ban
- Realized all the neighbors planted that easy-to-grow floozie in their flowerbeds too, even at the trailer park down the road
- Noted, with alarm, an army of that plant's offspring growing behind the football field.

Making plants play nice in places they aren't meant to grow requires unrealistic inputs of time, effort, water, fertilizers, chemical pesticides and the like. These are signs of problem plants, and when a popular plant becomes a problem, it's time for an intervention—it's time for plant problem-solvers, those unsung heroes that don't just fit the bill, they upgrade the garden.

Growing an engaging, original garden means choosing original plants. Instead of problem plants, consider these problem-solvers:

- Plants that tolerate summer heat and winter cold, even in the most rugged garden
- Plants with vibrant color, tantalizing texture, and elegant structure virtually year-round
- Plants that attract birds and bees, benefiting both their ecosystem and ours
- Plants that require less water
- Plants that aren't necessarily popular today, but will mature into the true garden originals of tomorrow.

The problem-solvers in these pages grow into more sustainable plants in every way. They're meant to be not only more environmentally sound than the popular problem children, but also more bountiful, more original, lower-care plants that are easier to grow and enjoy for gardeners of all levels of proficiency, practice, and time to devote to them.

It's time to grow up. Let's pretend the garden reunion is right around the corner. It's time to ditch the prom queens of the garden and upgrade with all-star problem-solvers.

17

Spikes of fleece flower (*Persicaria affinis*) replace those
of astilbe (*Astilbe*) in sunny spots.

How to Choose All-Star Plants

You've seen it across the nursery yard, planted smugly in its well-watered pot of synthetic, slow-release fertilizer, its come-hither flowers beckoning beneath lustrous leaves. You know your love is forbidden—it's a problem plant waiting to happen. Don't be seduced! Dozens of more satisfying, more sustainable all-star solutions are rubbing elbows with those troublemakers right there at your nursery. But with so many plants to choose from, how do you weed out the Lotharios from the winners?

This chapter breaks down that process into three parts:

1 Seduction

What exactly do you see in that problem plant? We'll look at key elements of design (and desire) that characterize plants. When you identify the ingredients of plant seduction, you've taken the first step toward picking a better plant to fall for.

2 Location

Your garden—who grows there? We'll define your site the way a plant would as a potential tenant. Understanding how plants see your garden helps further narrow the playing field, and it's an imperative second step.

3 Selection

It's finally time to shop, yet you're still completely overwhelmed by the options. All those jangly botanical names, all those different varieties. Which plant is right? We'll tie it all together with a short course on how best to get your hands around the winning plant you deserve.

The plants suggested in this book are the tip of the iceberg! The plant kingdom is full of star garden students ripe for the picking. With a little effort, you should be able to troubleshoot plant problems, zero in on solutions, and upgrade your garden with beautiful, bountiful, sustainable plants above and beyond the plants here. Follow me as we learn how to plant problem-solve from scratch.

Seduction: Connecting the Design Dots from Troublesome Seducer to All-Star Solution

The plant kingdom is a living lineup of sensuous characters. Plants enrich and inform our most treasured outdoor spaces—and many indoors too—with scent, sound, touch, and taste, and most importantly, with sight. Visually beautiful plants first beguiled their way into vogue in ancient times, and if there's a plant diva you wish you could grow, it's probably turned heads now for centuries.

But why is it you wish you could grow that plant? Odds are you're seduced by one of a few simple aesthetic qualities. We'll call these qualities elements of design.

Take a good look at that problem plant, batting its eyes across the nursery yard, and consider the following characteristics. Think of them like bits of personal ads for plants! Breaking down the pieces of what attracts us to plants will help us pick better plants to replace problems.

You'll notice each element of design, save for character, has a symbol. When these symbols are highlighted in entries for alternatives, that tells you it has qualities that overlap with the problem plant in terms of that design element.

COLOR

First, there's color, the most straightforward element of design. If there's one quality that defines the laws of plant attraction, it's color. It's fair to say we grow most plants (or wish we could) specifically for color, often flower color. But say a plant blooms in superfabulous hues seven days a year—what does it do for you the other fifty-one weeks? Is it fabulous in other ways, or is it a pouty, leafy lump that you stare at the rest of the year, all the while pining for that one week of bloom? If it's the latter, is that plant really worth your while?

In choosing a better plant, color shouldn't come but once a year, and if possible, it shouldn't come only in flower. Look for those superstar plants that twirl the color wheel again and again across the calendar year (even year-round!), and in foliage, fruit, bark, and any other way you can think of.

The colors we'll stick mostly to are those on the spokes of the wheel: *red, orange, yellow, green, blue*, and *violet*, as well as *white, tan,* and *brown,* three underrated colors that are just as important. Supporting colors that make frequent appearances include *pink, gold,* and *lavender.*

SHAPE

Next up, we find shape. In a nutshell, shape is how a plant works the room. You know basic shapes—circle, square, rectangle, triangle. Well, plants come in shapes too, and they're not too far off from these basics.

Seldom is shape the deciding factor in picking a plant, but the smart gardener knows shape is a major player in the big picture of any garden. How does that plant fill space through the year? A plant may not always be in leaf, and it may not always be blooming, but during the growing season and, for many, year-round, a plant's shape is what sells it.

Shape is that sneaky element of design that draws in so many gardeners without their realizing it, because it has the power to seduce on a more unconscious, sentimental level. Think about it: are you in love with a plant with big palm-shaped leaves? Could it be because its shapely silhouette conjures up images of that tropical vacation you took, even though that plant grows in your own untropical backyard?

Because this book is a jumping off point, be aware the term *shape* can be interpreted in different ways in landscape design. It's often discussed together with the terms *form*, a plant's shape in the big picture overall, and *habit*, the specific way a plant tends to grow. Don't let these terms trip you up! For our purposes, we'll roll them all into one, and for plants grown mostly for their flowers, we'll look specifically at flower shape.

Here's a list of the plant shapes we'll cover:

- **Trees**
  Columnar, conical, irregular, mounded, open, oval, pyramidal, rounded, spreading, upright, vase, weeping

- **Shrubs**
  Columnar, conical, irregular, mounded, open, oval, prostrate, pyramidal, rounded, spreading, symmetrical, upright, vase, weeping

- **Perennial Plant Shapes**
  Branching, clump, feather, mounded, paddle, rosette, rounded pad, spiky, upright

- **Perennial Flower Shapes**
  Bunch, cup, daisy, double, fan, plume, spike, spray, trumpet, wand

- **Vines**
  Tendril/twining, clinging, rambling

● Grasses and Groundcovers

Arching, clinging, clumping, creeping, mounded, prostrate, rosette, rounded, spreading (if a woody groundcover), upright, vase

TEXTURE

After shape comes texture. At its most basic, texture is the way you think a plant might feel if you touched it, based on how it looks. Texture is responsible for a plant's shimmer and sheen. Think of texture as plant jewelry. Though we seldom grow plants specifically for it, texture is a double-edged sword of seduction, because it speaks both to sight and to touch.

Grab that plant you love, and take a closer look at it. Are its leaves smooth like the surface of a mirror? We'd call those leaves *glossy*. But maybe instead they tame the sun's rays into many tiny bits of light. In that case, we'd say they were *soft*.

Step back and look at how your plant's surfaces—leaves, flowers, and all—play with light together. This speaks to its overall visual texture, and here's where design elements dovetail, because the gestalt of a plant's texture depends on the size and shape of all its pieces. An enormous tree with thousands of tiny leaves has a *fine* texture. Likewise, the texture of one with big, bodacious leaves is *bold*. Trees (and other plants) in the middle are, simply, *medium*.

Like shape, texture is a stealthy design element that doesn't often take center stage in plant pageantry, yet always plays a role. Texture done right has the potential to dazzle.

SIZE

Size is another somewhat obvious element of design, but don't let its factual nature fool you into thinking it's any less sexy. Untold numbers of plants rise to popularity simply because they're particularly titanic or particularly tiny.

The most important thing to realize about size is how it relates to your space. Whether you measure your garden in square feet or acres, a plant won't reach its full potential unless it has room to grow and thrive both in general and relative to the rest of the garden. Some plant prima donnas falter with too little space, and some pernicious plants overtake their neighbors. Neither will make you happy in the end.

Small spaces are a frequent concern for gardeners of today, and it just so happens a world of rock star plants are available to beautifully fill (not overfill) smaller niches where their linebacker counterparts may fail.

CHARACTER

Character is the final element of design to consider when selecting a plant for your garden. Character takes into account the plant in all its qualities—color, shape, texture, size—along with other, harder-to-define aspects, and answers the basic "why" in growing this particular plant. What will this plant will do for us? What role would we typically look to this plant to play in our gardens? Is it meant to be a big tree with great fall color, or a midsized perennial with flowers that smell great? Character, as used in this book, speaks to what's called for in space, time, and situation, and every garden needs a complete cast of characters. Unlike the school play, however, the garden works just fine without plants to act as antagonists.

An additional set of terms you'll see in character relate to how a plant changes through the year. Trees, shrubs, and woody groundcovers that lose their leaves in winter are referred to as *deciduous*. Perennials, vines, grasses, and groundcovers that maintain their leafiness though winter are called *evergreen*, those in between are *semievergreen*, and if they die back in the ground, they're *herbaceous*. Likewise, I'll talk about when a plant does the things we're most interested in, like whether it blooms in spring, if it has fetching *multiseason* foliage over a period of months, or if makes for an interesting visual presence *year-round*.

Relative to color and character, I'll point out whether particularly colorful plants stand out for foliage, flower, and even bark. One example might be *Deutzia* 'Chardonnay Pearls', which brightens up any space with its gold foliage. Another is *Stachys* 'Helene von Stein', a vision in silvery white.

Finally, I'll make special note of plants that play a few very defined roles gardeners always want to know about: those that work well as *hedges*, are *fragrant* or *edible*, and when plants that don't appear in the grasses and groundcover chapter work well as *groundcovers*.

Location: Defining Which Plants Can Grow in Your Garden

If the garden is the high school musical, then plants must be its cast of characters, and, of course, the cycle of seasons is its plot. Like every good play, then, every good garden must set the stage, and the bits and pieces that make up the garden's setting tell us what plants will grow best

there. Yep, you got it—even in the garden, the secret to all-star success can be about location, location, location.

Just like people, different plants need different things to grow. In this section, we'll define those growing needs and look at how they relate to your garden. After all, to understand which all-star plants will be most likely to succeed there, it's key to understand your garden not just as acreage, but also as plant habitat.

As with the design elements I talked about a moment ago, you'll notice symbols for hardiness and light, and when these are highlighted in entries for alternatives, that means they overlap with problem plants in terms of growing range and light requirements.

HARDINESS

Hardiness is the first growing need to consider in plant problem-solving. The term *hardiness* refers to how much cold a plant can weather. The U.S. Department of Agriculture's Hardiness Zone Map is the most widely accepted tool for determining the chill factor of your garden location.

The USDA map divides North America into ten hardiness zones by average low temperature, then divides them a step further, giving each zone an "a" and a "b" part. That way, gardeners can pinpoint within five degrees the average low temperature where they live.

When you're on the hunt for plant problem-solvers, make note of a plant's hardiness rating on its tag. If, for example, it says "Zones 5–10," you'll know that, in trials, that plant survived low temps from hardiness zone 5a (−15 to −20 degrees F/−26 to −29 degrees C) to 10b (35 to 40 degrees F/4 to 2 degrees C).

USDA Zones and Corresponding Temperatures

Temp °F	Zone	Temp°C	Temp °F	Zone	Temp°C
-60 to -55	1a	-51 to -48	5 to 10	7b	-15 to -12
-55 to -50	1b	-48 to -46	10 to 15	8a	-12 to -9
-50 to -45	2a	-46 to -43	15 to 20	8b	-9 to -7
-45 to -40	2b	-43 to -40	20 to 25	9a	-7 to -4
-40 to -35	3a	-40 to -37	25 to 30	9b	-4 to -1
-35 to -30	3b	-37 to -34	30 to 35	10a	-1 to 2
-30 to -25	4a	-34 to -32	35 to 40	10b	2 to 4
-25 to -20	4b	-32 to -29	40 to 45	11a	4 to 7
-20 to -15	5a	-29 to -26	45 to 50	11b	7 to 10
-15 to -10	5b	-26 to -23	50 to 55	12a	10 to 13
-10 to -5	6a	-23 to -21	55 to 60	12b	13 to 16
-5 to 0	6b	-21 to -18	60 to 65	13a	16 to 18
0 to 5	7a	-18 to -15	65 to 70	13b	18 to 21

Find your hardiness zone on the map and compare it to the zone(s) in which that plant you've had your eye on is rated to grow. If your zone doesn't fall within that plant's range, it's a no-go. Guess what, though? There are all-stars for all zones.

For our purposes, we'll be talking about hardiness in whole zones and only break things down into "a" and "b" zones if a plant's winter hardiness is a bit unproven, or *marginal*.

It's also important to know that even if a plant is "zone hardy," all zones are not created equal. Heat and humidity are supporting players in the garden setting. After all, Zone 6 in cool Massachusetts, a location where relative humidity and precipitation are high, is a far cry from Zone 6 in the high, dry desert of New Mexico. Right now, there's no tool as accepted as the USDA Zone Map for determining a plant's penchant for heat, but we'll talk about heat and humidity in the big picture and what they might be like where you live in a moment. A basic awareness of climate will go a long way toward helping you pick the right problem-solver in terms of heat, cold, and hardiness zone.

LIGHT

Light is just as important on the garden stage as it is in theater, and it's the next growing need of plants to consider. If you're choosing a plant for a certain spot, keep an eye on that spot for the next few days. Does it get *full sun* (five to six hours or more of sunlight per day), *part shade* to *part sun* (three to four hours), or *full shade* (one or two hours or less)? Lots of plants also grow great in *light shade*, which means filtered or reflected sunlight for much of the day—light that shines through the branches of tall trees, for example.

Now take a look at the light requirements for the plant you wish you could grow. If it's a sun-worshipper and you garden in a shady location, or vice versa, it's probably time to search for a problem-solving plant. All plants get their energy through photosynthesis, a process for which sunlight is required. Some plants need more of it, and some thrive on less.

Sun is also a hot-button issue—literally. With sun comes heat, and while some plants may like it sunny, they may not like it hot. Because the sun's rays tend to be more kind in the morning, some all-star plants do better with a little shade in the heat of the day.

WATER AND SOIL

Water and soil are two plant growing needs that are inextricably linked, like star-crossed lovers. Let's cover water first. All plants need water to survive, but some need more than others, and water isn't as abundant in some places as it is in others.

Plants need water especially during the growing season, when they're actively packing on roots and shoots. How much average rainfall does your garden get when plants are at their growing peak? Would that plant you wanted to grow wilt if you couldn't water it enough? You'll need to water even the most drought-tolerant plants for a time when they're newly planted to get them settled in, but if an established plant continues to wilt dramatically without lots of water, odds are there's a low-water all-star that would be happier with the amount of water that falls naturally from the sky where you live.

Water is also a bit player in the garden setting in the form of humidity. Some plants falter when too little moisture reaches their roots. Others can't hack the heat index when high temps mix with high air moisture, transforming your garden into a blistering steam room. Still other plants thrive in humidity and can't take dry air.

Which is it in your garden—too much water or too little?

If your garden is located near a river or stream, you may deal with water in a different form—the kind that saturates the ground. Where water meets ground, we need to talk about soil, the most complex character in the play of a plant's growing needs.

Water and soil both play roles in *drainage*. If you find it's mucky not too far below the surface of your garden's soil, or if water pools for days or weeks in your garden when it rains, you definitely have *wet soil*, also known as soil that doesn't drain well. Wet soils occur near bodies of water or places where water pools—rivers, ponds, lakes, and streams.

While boggy conditions can be a challenge for some plants, many plants actually prefer *moist soil*, a step down in dampness from wet. Since water helps with the breakdown of organic matter—what gardeners know as that good stuff that comes from great compost, for example, or decaying leaves or bark mulch—nutrients tend to be more readily available for uptake by a plant's roots.

Dry soil can be more challenging. If you garden in a location where water doesn't reach or collect readily in the topsoil—a sunny hillside or under a dense canopy of mature trees, for example—you may deal with soil that dries out more quickly. Most plants do fine in *average soil*, a compromise between wet and dry, and the majority of plants at nurseries will have tags that tell you they prefer soil that's *well-drained*. Translation: they like water, but they'd rather not sit in it or go months without it.

But wait—there's more to soil and drainage than meets the eye. Soil's role as a complex character also lies in its makeup. Is your soil clay? Is it sand? Is it more like loam, with plenty of organic matter? You'll find all-star solutions that do well in each soil type, and each has its own quirks.

Clay soil, for example, gets mucky and doesn't drain well when it rains. It also hardens to a plant-killing crust during drought. But guess what? Clay is high in the nutrients that plants love. It may need to be worked a bit to unlock those nutrients and improve how it drains.

In contrast, sand wants nothing to do with water or nutrients—water runs right through it. Sandy and rocky soils often are lean, drain fast, and leave plants holding the bag. The good news is that plenty of plants love these lean soils, too.

Loamy soil is the type in which most gardens grow most readily. The secret to loam's success lies in its diversity of particles—some tiny, like clay, and some big, like sand—as well as plenty of organic matter, breaking down and providing good stuff for the ecosystems of tiny life that exist in all soils, as well as plants.

Soil pH, a measure of soil acidity or alkalinity, can be a big deal too, as it influences a plant's ability to absorb nutrients. Some plants, like those that have adapted to live under the canopies of conifers, would much rather grow in *acidic soil*. Others, particularly many desert plants, prefer *alkaline soil*. Soil pH is measured on a scale from 0 to 14, with 7 being neutral. A rule of thumb is that soils higher in organic matter that's breaking down tend to be more acidic, while soils that are low in organic matter are more alkaline.

Confused yet? Don't worry! There are a few easy ways to unearth your soil's potential.

First, read up on the typical soil in your part of the country. I'll talk about this in general terms in a moment, but soil trends certain directions in different regions.

Next, get a soil test—a real one, not a DIY kit from a store. Odds are a nearby college or university has a lab that does soil testing. It's as simple as sending them a baggie with a form, and voila! They'll reply with a wealth of information on your soil and what grows there, including its composition in terms of sand, loam, clay, organic matter, and other things, as well as pH. They'll also tell you whether it's worth attempting to amend your soil—that is, adding various components like organic matter to help plants grow better. (If you find yourself constantly amending your soil, perhaps you're attempting to grow the wrong plants. See the "Maintenance" section up next.)

Finally, do a bit of detective work. Dig up a handful of soil from your garden and work it into a ball. Is it mucky and wet? If it is, it's safe to say you have wet soil, or at least soil that won't drain well. Does it crumble to dust in your hands before it can be worked? It's definitely dry. If it's something in between—maybe a bit damp, but it holds together—you've got average soil. Likewise, you can get a sense of the amount of organic matter in your soil simply based on how much stuff you see in it—and that stuff includes things like decaying leaves and other plant material, as well as living stuff like earthworms and other critters.

Whatever your soil situation, you can be sure there are plants that will thrive in it. It's just a matter of finding the all-stars that suit your garden.

MAINTENANCE

The last of a plant's growing needs is one most gardeners might not consider after thinking about hardiness, light, soil, and water. Maintenance, however, is vitally important to some plants. After all, if no one's building the sets for the play of the garden, the whole production falls apart.

What is maintenance? Maintenance is pruning, watering, mulching, amending the soil, raking leaves, and mowing the lawn. It's is everything you have to do to keep your garden going. It takes time, and a lot of people resent it, including me.

Maintenance is so important for many garden plants because they've been bred to live solely in your gardens. Plants can't prune or mow or spray themselves for bugs, so these tasks fall to you. In the world of garden plants, maintenance can be as key to survival as any other growing need, but while the other factors we've discussed come part and parcel with a garden's location, maintenance is down to you. It's your garden—how much work will you put into it?

Maintenance is a touchy topic in this busy day and age, as well it should be. Many a popular problem plant whose mug shot appears in these pages is a poster child for high maintenance. While the all-stars I've chosen are, as a rule, vastly less work to maintain, the "no maintenance garden" is wishful thinking. Most plants need at least a small bit of care at some time in their lives, and while many problem-solvers may be low maintenance, the zero-maintenance garden is a myth.

GEOGRAPHY

Remember when I mentioned different regions set the stage for the garden play in different ways? Here's a breakdown of those regions, moving clockwise around the continent.

The *Northeast* and *Midwest* stretch roughly from the Great Lakes to the East Coast, and feature cold winters and summers that are hot and humid, but relatively mild compared to neighboring regions. All-star plants should enjoy moisture year-round—below-freezing winters with frozen ground and snow that segues to rain in spring. Summers aren't as soggy, but they come with thunderstorms. Areas along coastlines are cooler and drier in summer because of wind, and milder in winter. Everything gets more extreme away from the coasts, with hotter summers and colder winters. Since these cold-weather regions are also home to lots of deciduous trees that lose their leaves, the soil tends to be high in organic matter and more acidic.

The same goes for soil pH in the *Southeast*, much of which has the added bonus of an abundance of red clay. If there's one thing a southern gardener knows, it's that climate here tends to be humid year-round. Winters are mild and wet, and temps may dip below freezing, but not so much that the ground freezes. Summers are the pressure cooker of seasons, with extreme heat coupled with high humidity. Thunderstorms bring periodic relief. All-star plants have to take the heat and wet, as well as soils that may not drain so readily.

Following along, we come to the *Southwest*, where climate transitions from humid to arid, and as tree cover becomes less common, soil transitions from acidic to alkaline. Winters are mild but chilly, and this is when the region gets most of its rainfall. Summers are hot, hot, hot, with high humidity in eastern portions of Texas—where it's more likely to rain some in summer—that tapers off into the dry heat of the true deserts of New Mexico, Arizona, and southwestern California. All-star plants must be able to withstand drought and thrive in soils that are lower in nutrients.

The *West Coast* trends from dry to wet. Coastal regions of California see Mediterranean climates, with cool, mild winters when rainfall is plenty, and dry summers with low humidity and little to no rain. Summer temps range from mild to hot, with more extreme heat inland. All-star plants here need to handle prolonged periods of drought. Up the coast in the Pacific Northwest, drought becomes less of a concern as the climate turns to maritime. Summer temps become mild, and there's rainfall aplenty year-round. Warm ocean currents make winters wet, but usually mild as well.

The *Mountains* region includes the area from the mountains of the West Coast to the Rockies, and just on the other side. Between the mountain ranges, winters are cold and wet and summers dry, with areas of high desert and low humidity. Here, all-star plants have to deal with

extremes of temperature and lack of moisture. Soil can be lean, and higher elevations bring dry air—just as valleys are a bit more temperate, because moister air pools in lower-lying places.

Finally, the *Great Plains* are a return to more extreme seasons as you move from west to east—perhaps the most extreme in terms of shift. East of the Rockies, in the vast plains at the center of North America, humidity returns, and with it summers can be a steam bath. Winters can be similarly damp, with excesses of snow, but they can be dry as well, especially in the southern plains. Though all-stars here must deal with these extremes, the plains are blessed with some of the continent's richest soils, and plants benefit from that.

Now that you've found your location in the great setting of the garden drama, it's finally time to pick the players.

Selection: Making Sense of the Options

You did it! You looked that problem plant square in the face and demanded better. You discovered the stage your garden sets and are ready for all-star solutions to match. At long last, the time has come to choose the fabulous plant to replace that troublesome stinker.

You go to the nursery. . . And find you're still overwhelmed at the options. What happened?

It's an all-too-frequent story: many gardeners throw in the towel when it comes time to shop. You either give up because of the mind-boggling selection, or you forget everything you've learned and go off on a plant-buying frenzy that just feels wrong the following day.

Shopping is supposed to be the fun part—the answers lie in the options.

Think of the nursery, like the garden, as the set of the school play. You'll find directors, that is, customer service folks to help you; producers, more behind-the-scenes personnel who grow and care for plants; and, of course, actors—the plants themselves.

Just like a play has different types of actors, the nursery, and eventually your garden, has plants that perform different roles. Plants that seem interesting, but may not be as attractive or dramatic as to garner a lead role, are the character actors at the nursery. Then there are a whole lot of extras, whose presence is still integral, including annuals, plants that only appear this season. Finally, there are the lead actors, the most visually attractive, fabulously displayed plants. These leading actors will have stunt doubles. At the nursery, lead plant actors will sometimes have dozens of doubles, each with a different name!

It may be obvious that the role of all-star in your garden will go to a lead nursery player, but sometimes, you'll need to choose from among a group of equally attractive doubles. Quite often, one of the character actors might suit your production better, growing into a leading lady once it's planted in your garden. How to make sense of it all?

PLANT NAMES

When you set foot in a nursery, will it be like stepping into a romantic comedy or an ill-advised trip down the basement stairs on a dark, stormy night? The difference between the two lies in plant names. No, not the everyday *common names* we use, like sugar maple and aster, but the *botanical names* of those plants, including genus, species, and possibly cultivar.

Many new gardeners dread the point at which they have to walk into a nursery and ask for a plant by its botanical name. Guess what? It's time to learn to let go of your inhibitions about botanical names. The reason is that botanical names will be a powerful tool in identifying your plant when you go to buy it.

Common names will only get you so far, because common names equal confusion. Different kinds of plants will often have the same common name, and different people may use different common names for the same plant. For example, if you ask someone at a nursery or do a web search for *geranium*, you're likely to find dozens of different kinds of plants that might not be right for you. If, however, you head into the plant world to shop for a geranium by the name of *Geranium macrorrhizum* 'Bevan's Variety', that is what you'll get. Ask and ye shall receive!

What does all that botanical naming *mean* anyway? And how do you pronounce it? And what if you say it wrong?

Here's the thing: you don't need to *speak* the language to use it to shop for plants. You need only be aware of a plant's botanical name. It's as simple as running a web search for that name, or writing it down so you can show it to someone at the nursery when you get there.

If you find you need to sound the name out to explain what you're after, you're in good company: nine times out of ten, the person helping you at the nursery will be muddling through botanical name pronunciation too, but they'll have abandoned any concerns that they're saying it wrong long ago. You'll give a college try at *Symphyotrichum novae-angliae* 'Purple Dome', they'll do the same, you'll both chuckle, and then you'll find what you're looking for.

That said, it's a good idea to have a very basic knowledge of what plant names mean, so let's do a little decoding. Here's what you really need to know:

The first word in a plant's name—*Symphyotrichum*, in our example—is the name of its *genus*. A genus is a group of plants that are similar. Think of a genus as a close-knit family. For a handful of all-stars in this book, I'll recommend a whole genus of plants, because so many family members are great that it's nearly impossible to go wrong.

More often, I'll recommend a specific family member within that genus. That's a *species*. A plant's species name is the second word in its botanical names. *Symphyotrichum novae-angliae*, for example, refers to a specific plant (*novae-angliae*) within the genus *Symphyotrichum*.

What, then, are all those words, a lot of which seem to be everyday words in English, which show up in single quotes after a plant's botanical name? Those are the last piece of the plant name puzzle, the name of a specific *cultivar* of that plant. Even within a species, there can be plants that show all kinds of different characteristics—variegated leaves, yellow flowers instead of red, or a skinnier shape, for example. Often, when these plants are discovered, plant breeders cultivate them to play up those characteristics. When that happens, a cultivar is born, and it's given a name. *Symphyotrichum novae-angliae* 'Purple Dome' is an aster cultivar that's cultivated for its purple flower and neat, mounded shape.

Not too hard, right? Now let's talk about your shopping experience. After all, if you want to find that all-star garden plant, you might need a little help.

SHOPPING

Hands down, nurseries will be your go-to source for plant knowledge. Nursery personnel work among plants day in and day out. At the very least, they've been trained in plant basics—at most, they're professional horticulturists with a treasure trove of information to share.

More than that, the average nursery customer is usually interested in the popular problem plant that you want to be rid of, and guess what? Knowledgeable nursery folk would rather be rid of the troublemakers, too. They're usually thrilled to discover an interested customer who wants to dig a bit deeper. If you're really curious to learn more about plants, look for that nursery horticulturist whose eyes light up when they get that. Odds are that person is someone from whom you can learn.

If you don't find your plant at your local nursery, don't be shy about asking if they can order it. Often it's no trouble, especially when it comes to trees and shrubs. Often it won't cost more to order a plant than if you'd found it there in the first place, and it'll usually be bigger than if you get it mail order.

Big box stores have become popular places to shop for plants, and they come with advantages and disadvantages. For customers who are confident in their ability to find what they're looking for, big box stores offer many garden mainstays and often at a lower price. The less assured shopper, however, should be wary. While the big boxes may be a decent source for the basics, too often their personnel are less knowledgeable. Because of that, they won't have the same expertise as nursery workers, they can't help you with questions, and their plants may suffer as a result.

Can't find that plant at your local nursery or the big boxes? You're in luck, because the internet has proven a boon to mail-order nurseries. In the back of this book, you'll find a list of better purveyors of plants through the web. Most are nurseries just like yours locally, complete with knowledgeable personnel, and most include a wealth of information and advice about the plants they sell on their web sites.

Mail-order plants have a reputation for being small, and they may require a bit more patience while they fill out, but you'll be surprised at the number of gallon-sized plants readily available to be shipped. If a plant grows slowly, try to buy it in person first, but if it's a fast-growing plant, smaller mail-order plants can sometimes be a cheaper alternative.

Three web sites will aid in your search: the University of Minnesota's Plant Information Online (plantinfo.umn.edu) provides links both to mail-order sources for plants and more information on them. PlantFiles from Dave's Garden (davesgarden.com/guides/pf) and Plant Lust (plantlust.com) also include links to mail-order plant sellers, as well as information on thousands of plants of all kinds. A neighbor of PlantFiles, Garden Watchdog (davesgarden.com/products/gwd) allows users to rate those vendors, so you can read up on the company you're buying from.

It's as simple as that! Are you ready to shop? Without further ado, let's move on to the plants themselves.

• •

Everyday Problem Plants and Extraordinary Alternatives

Vine maple (*Acer circinatum*) brings all the benefits of a native plant that Japanese maple (*Acer palmatum*) can't.

Where it's cold, the spring display of redbud (*Cercis canadensis*) gives jacaranda a run for its money.

34

Trees

Trees are the big kids in the schoolyard of the garden, but they need not be bullies. Their effect can either be boom—sensually interesting and exciting year-round, a boon to native wildlife—or bust—a constant source of litter from above, roots that make it hard for anything else to grow below. Many trees need plenty of water too, impossible in some climates. Let's look at a group of popular trees that make trouble, as well as all-stars that step up to the plate as trees that truly please.

35

BANANA

Musa species / *Ensete* species

- 🌡 Hardiness: **Zones (8)9–11**
- 🌲 Shape: **Open, upright**
- 🍃 Color: **Green or red leaf**
- ▦ Texture: **Bold**
- ☀ Light: **Full sun**
- 🔧 Size: **6–20 ft. high, 4–10 ft. wide**

Character:
Small evergreen tree grown for bold texture

The Carmen Miranda of plants, banana beats out all others for tropicality with its huge, paddle-shaped leaves. Though tree-sized, banana is a huge, fleshy perennial and best comes into its own in tropical climates. Few survive in cooler climates, but where they do, the whole "tree" dies to the ground each winter—leaves, trunks, and all—and makes for seriously messy cleanup.

CATALPA

Catalpa cultivars

Hardiness:
Zones 5–9

Shape:
Open, spreading

Color:
Green, gold, or purple leaf

Texture:
Bold

Light:
Full sun to part shade

Size:
If pruned to the ground, 6–8 ft. high, 6 ft. wide

Character:
Small deciduous tree grown for bold texture, multiseason gold or purple foliage in cultivars

Traditionally, catalpa grew in gardens as a huge tree, but today this unsung all-star is more often cut to the ground in late winter, spurring new growth of 6- to 8-foot shoots in spring, with enormous, bold leaves. Gold-leaved 'Aurea' (pictured) and purple-leaved 'Purpurea' make stupendous color displays.

UMBRELLA MAGNOLIA / BIGLEAF MAGNOLIA

Magnolia tripetala / Magnolia macrophylla

Hardiness: **Zones 5–9**	Texture: **Bold**
Shape: **Open, spreading**	Light: **Full sun to part shade**
Color: **Green leaf, white flower, red fruit**	Size: **30–40 ft. high and wide**

Character:
Small deciduous tree grown for bold texture, white spring flower, red fall fruit

Two hardy eastern natives for bodacious foliage, umbrella magnolia (pictured) and bigleaf magnolia make fast-growing tropicalesque accents as far north as Zone 5. The latter grows leaves up to 30 inches long, while the former's foliage tops out at 20. Both need a little simple pruning to look their best, and both appreciate some protection from heat and wind.

BANANA

LOQUAT

Eriobotrya japonica

Hardiness:
Zones 8–11

Shape:
Rounded

Color:
**Green leaf,
white flower,
gold fruit**

Texture:
Bold, glossy

Light:
**Full sun to
part shade**

Size:
**10–25 ft.
high and wide**

Character:
**Small evergreen tree or large shrub
grown for bold texture, fragrant white
fall flower; edible gold spring fruit**

Evergreen loquat looks tropical year-round, pushes well into frost-prone zones in its northern range, and produces fragrant flowers and edible fruit where frost is minimal. Loquat's leathery leaves handle wind better than lots of other big-leaved plants, and it stands up to drought once established. (Regular water will help it to fruit better.)

BAY

Laurus nobilis

🌡	Hardiness:	**Zones 8–10**
🍃	Shape:	**Rounded**
🖌	Color:	**Green leaf, yellow flower**
#	Texture:	**Medium**
☀	Light:	**Full sun to part shade**
📏	Size:	**10–30 ft. high, 5–20 ft. wide**

Character:

Small evergreen tree or large shrub grown for year-round fragrant foliage, mounded shape, as hedge

Bay, or true laurel, is a Mediterranean tree of antiquity, bearer of the laurel wreaths worn by ancient Greeks. Those aromatic leaves will be familiar to cooks too. Bay is valued as a prim and proper small tree, often used in topiary, but isn't a fan of cold climates and won't grow north of Zone 8.

BAYBERRY

Myrica pensylvanica

Hardiness:
Zones 3–7

Shape:
Open, mounded

Color:
Green leaf, blue berry

Texture:
Medium, glossy

Light:
Full sun to part shade

Size:
5–10 ft. high and wide

Character:
Small evergreen tree or large shrub grown for year-round fragrant foliage, blue fruit, mounded shape, as hedge

Rugged and cold-hardy, bayberry is a Boy Scout of plants, native to coastal areas of the Northeast. It tolerates drought and salt, grows fragrant leaves and steel blue berries prized by birds. Single or grouped, bayberry makes a straight-A garden addition. Male and female plants are a must for berry production.

39

BAY

'OTTO LUYKEN' ENGLISH LAUREL

Prunus laurocerasus 'Otto Luyken'

Hardiness: **Zones 6–8**	Texture: **Medium, glossy**
Shape: **Rounded, mounded**	Light: **Full sun to part shade**
Color: **Green leaf, white flower**	Size: **6–10 ft. high, 10–12 ft. wide**

Character:
Small evergreen tree or large shrub grown for year-round foliage, mounded shape, as hedge, fragrant white spring flower

Another hardy "laurel" that's neat as a pin is English laurel, a shrub or small tree with glossy, dark green leaves and fragrant white spring flowers. Star student 'Otto Luyken' is more compact and works well as a hedge. You may not notice fruit produced after flowering, but birds love it.

STAR ANISE

Illicium species

Hardiness:
Zones (6)7–10

Shape:
Rounded

Color:
**Green leaf,
red, yellow,
or pink flower**

Texture:
Medium, glossy

Light:
**Full sun to
part shade**

Size:
**6–10 ft. high,
6–8 ft. wide**

Character:
**Small evergreen tree or large shrub
grown for year-round fragrant
foliage, summer flower, as hedge**

"Star anise" covers several species of *Illicium*
native to North America and Asia. Hardy to
Zone 7, all bear awesomely anise-scented
leaves and outrageous flowers, each like a tiny
octopus. Southern native Florida star anise
(*I. floridanum*) blooms fire-engine red, *I.
anisatum* soft yellow, and *I. henryi* in pink.
Note: fruit of these species is not edible.

● ● ● ● ● ● ● ● ● ● ● ● ● ● ● ● ●

BIRCH

Betula papyrifera

🌡	Hardiness:	**Zones 2–6**
🌿	Shape:	**Open to weeping**
🖌	Color:	**White bark, yellow fall leaf**
▦	Texture:	**Medium, glossy**
☼	Light:	**Part sun to part shade**
📏	Size:	**50–70 ft. high, 25–50 ft. wide**

Character:
Small to medium deciduous tree grown for white bark, yellow fall foliage

In the birch family, paper birch is the kid whose parents expect too much. This birch adores bitter cold, but its gorgeous white bark sees it planted in gardens far warmer than it likes. The result? Struggling, short-lived trees and the spread of bronze birch borer, an insect pest that inhabits those warmer zones too.

LONDON PLANE

Platanus ×acerifolia

Hardiness:	Texture:
Zones 4–9	**Medium to bold**

Shape:	Light:
Open to rounded	**Full sun**

Color:	Size:
Brown, gray, and white bark	**75–100 ft. high, 60–75 ft. wide**

Character:
Large deciduous tree grown for brown, gray, and white bark, open shape

A classic tree, mature London plane's corky brown bark chips off to reveal creamy white underneath. Adaptable, long-lived, and tough as nails, London plane is a hybrid of native American sycamore (*Platanus occidentalis*) and Asian plane (*P. orientalis*). It gets big in gardens and grows more slowly, albeit happily, as a street tree.

43

BIRCH

SEVEN-SON FLOWER

Heptacodium miconioides

Hardiness:
Zones 4–9

Texture:
Medium

Shape:
Open, irregular to rounded

Light:
Full sun to part shade

Color:
White bark, white to pink flower, pink fruit

Size:
15–20 ft. high, 8–10 ft. wide

Character:
Small deciduous tree or large shrub grown for white bark, white to pink fall flower, pink fall fruit

Seven-son flower wins "Most Likely to Succeed" in trees and shrubs: peeling white bark, glossy green leaves, and fragrant white flowers in fall, followed by pink-purple fruit and calyces—the outer parts of the flower. It's a showstopper in small gardens and patios, and thrives in a range of conditions.

NEW MEXICO PRIVET

Forestiera pubescens var. *neomexicana*

Hardiness:
Zones 4–9

Shape:
Vase

Color:
**White bark,
gold fall leaf**

Texture:
**Medium to
fine, glossy**

Light:
**Full sun to
part shade**

Size:
**15 ft. high
and wide**

Character:
**Small deciduous tree grown for white
bark, as hedge, gold fall foliage**

A Southwest native, New Mexico privet thrives
in desert conditions, and birds love the blue
berries of female plants. Lower branches can
be pruned away to make it a small tree and
show off its white bark, or it can be left shaggy
for a more naturalistic look.

45

BLUE SPRUCE

Picea pungens

	Hardiness:	**Zones 2–7**
	Shape:	**Upright to pyramidal**
	Color:	**Blue leaf**
	Texture:	**Fine, soft**
	Light:	**Full sun**
	Size:	**30–60 ft. high, 10–20 ft. wide**

Character:
Large evergreen tree grown for year-round blue foliage, pyramidal shape, fine texture

Colorado blue spruce is busy staring out the classroom window, wishing it were growing in the mountains, not your hot, humid garden. If it's an unhappy tree, it's a disease-prone tree. Colorado blue gets big too—bigger than many a gardener hoping for an "outdoor Christmas tree" may realize.

WHITE FIR

Abies concolor

Hardiness:
Zones 3–7

Shape:
Upright to pyramidal

Color:
Blue leaf

Texture:
Fine, soft

Light:
Full sun to part shade

Size:
50–70 ft. high, 20–30 ft. wide

Character:
Large evergreen tree grown for year-round blue foliage, pyramidal shape, fine texture

An all-star blue-needled conifer with a misleading name, white fir works better in heat and drought than Colorado blue spruce, resists disease, and takes a touch of shade too. Its flattened needles also make it a more touchable tree than the prickly blue spruce it replaces.

JAPANESE FIR

Abies firma

Hardiness:	Texture:
Zones 5–8	**Fine, soft**

Shape:	Light:
Pyramidal	**Full sun**

Color:	Size:
Dark green leaf	**20–30 ft. tall,** **10–15 ft. wide**

Character:
Small evergreen tree grown for year-round foliage, pyramidal shape, fine texture

Classic-looking conifers can be hard to come by in the heat of the Southeast. Among them, Japanese fir adapts to heat, some drought, and even a measure of poorly draining clay soil. It fits well into smaller gardens, and its clean, green silhouette should satisfy conifer fans south to Zone 8.

BLUE SPRUCE

ARIZONA CYPRESS

Cupressus arizonica

Hardiness:
Zones 7–11

Shape:
Pyramidal

Color:
Blue leaf

Texture:
Fine, soft

Light:
Full sun

Size:
30–40 ft. high, 15–20 ft. wide

Character:
Small evergreen tree grown for year-round blue foliage, pyramidal shape, fine texture

A native of the Southwest, Arizona cypress scores in hot, dry climates where other conifers might bake, and it adapts fairly well in humid regions, too. This cypress grows fast to tree size and makes good shelter for birds. Flashy cultivars 'Blue Ice' (pictured) and 'Blue Pyramid' sport shimmery, silver-blue foliage.

CALLERY PEAR

Pyrus calleryana and cultivars

🌡	Hardiness:	**Zones 5–9**
🌳	Shape:	**Oval, mounded**
🔧	Color:	**White flower, red-purple fall leaf**
♯	Texture:	**Medium, glossy**
☼	Light:	**Full sun**
📏	Size:	**25–35 ft. high, 20–25 ft. wide**

Character:
Small deciduous tree grown for mounded shape, white spring flower, red fall foliage

Callery pear is a real stinker, especially its flowers in spring, but also for a weak branch structure prone to breaking. It's an invasive species in parts of the country too. A popular street tree, its tidiness and terrific fall color belie these qualities. This tree is trouble with a capital *P*.

LITTLELEAF LINDEN

Tilia cordata

Hardiness:
Zones 4–8

Shape:
Pyramidal to oval, mounded

Color:
Yellow flower, gold fall leaf

Texture:
Medium, glossy

Light:
Full sun to part shade

Size:
50–70 ft. high, 35–50 ft. wide

Character:
Small to medium deciduous tree grown for mounded shape, fragrant yellow spring flower, yellow fall foliage

All-star littleleaf linden adapts well most any place and makes a sensational street tree. It's tough and tidy, and the heady fragrance of its summer blooms attracts both pollinators and people. Autumn foliage is a stately gold. Littleleaf linden makes a backdrop of crisp dark green during the growing season.

CALLERY PEAR

TUPELO

Nyssa sylvatica

Hardiness:
Zones 3–9

Shape:
Pyramidal to rounded, mounded

Color:
Orange to red fall leaf

Texture:
Medium, glossy

Light:
Full sun to part shade

Size:
30–50 ft. high, 20–30 ft. wide

Character:
Small to medium deciduous tree grown for orange to red fall foliage, mounded shape

An adaptable eastern native, low-care tupelo thrives in a huge range of climates and soil types, and its glossy green foliage turns to a crazy quilt of color in fall. Spring flowers, though you might not see them, bring bees from miles around. Tupelo grows a deep taproot, so site it with care in a location for the long-term.

'MARINA' STRAWBERRY TREE

Arbutus 'Marina'

Hardiness:
Zones 8–10

Texture:
Medium, glossy

Shape:
Rounded to open, mounded

Light:
Full sun

Color:
Pink flower, red fruit, red bark

Size:
20–40 ft. high and wide

Character:
Small evergreen tree grown for multiseason pink flower and fruit, red bark, mounded shape

'Marina' strawberry tree makes multiseason beauty look easy: pink flowers are followed by red fruit, while red bark turns cinnamon and peels in late summer. Compact in form and glossy in leaf, if trained to a single trunk, 'Marina' makes a delectable, drought-resistant street tree.

CITRUS

Citrus species

🌡	Hardiness:	**Zones 9–11**
🌳	Shape:	**Rounded**
🖌	Color:	**Orange, yellow, or green fruit, white flower**
▦	Texture:	**Medium**
☼	Light:	**Full sun**
📏	Size:	**10–15 ft. high, 8–10 ft. wide**

Character:
Small evergreen tree or large shrub grown for edible summer fruit, fragrant white spring flower

Orange, lemon, lime, and more—the flamboyant citrus sisters' flirtation with humans dates back to ancient times. Beloved almost as much for sweetly fragrant flowers as fruit, few citrus trees truly grow well outside frost-free climates.

HARDY ORANGE

Poncirus trifoliata

Hardiness:
Zones 5–9

Shape:
Rounded

Color:
Yellow fruit, white flower

Texture:
Medium

Light:
Full sun to light shade

Size:
8–20 ft. high, 6–15 ft. wide

Character:
Small deciduous tree or large shrub grown for fragrant white spring flower, yellow summer fruit

Hardy orange is the tough chick that takes up where its cold-fearing cousins leave off. Easily grown in a variety of soils as far north as Zone 5, this prickly beauty has outsized ornamental thorns, and prunes into an excellent small tree, with fragrant blossoms to boot. Fruit is bitter but sweetly scented, better dried for potpourri than eaten.

LEWIS' MOCK ORANGE

Philadelphus lewisii

Hardiness:
Zones 3–9

Texture:
Medium

Shape:
Vase to rounded

Light:
Full sun to part shade

Color:
White flower, gray bark

Size:
6–8 ft. high and wide

Character:
Small deciduous tree or large shrub grown for fragrant white spring flower, gray bark

Western native Lewis' mock orange grows into a huge, multistemmed shrub. Prune branches from its base to reveal its pretty, peely trunks. Add to that cold-hardiness and fragrant white spring flowers, and you've got a winner. Intensely fragrant 'Cheyenne' is especially drought tolerant.

53

CITRUS

54

MEYER LEMON

Citrus ×meyeri

Hardiness: **Zones (8)9–11**	Texture: **Medium**
Shape: **Rounded**	Light: **Full sun to part shade**
Color: **White flower, yellow fruit**	Size: **6–10 ft. high and wide**

Character:
Small evergreen tree or large shrub grown for yellow summer fruit, fragrant white spring flowers

Meyer lemon is the hardiest and heartiest citrus tree. More frost-tolerant than its peers, it grows well in protected areas as far north as Zone 8, blooms with abandon, and makes edible fruit to boot. Meyer lemon even shines for northern gardeners in containers.

● ● ● ● ● ● ● ● ● ● ● ● ● ● ● ● ● ● ●

DOGWOOD

Cornus florida

	Hardiness:	**Zones 5–9**
	Shape:	**Open to rounded**
	Color:	**White or pink flower, red fall leaf**
	Texture:	**Medium**
	Light:	**Full sun to part shade**
	Size:	**15–30 ft. high and wide**

Character:

Medium deciduous tree grown for white or pink spring flower, red fall foliage

A pouty spring-blooming beauty, flowering dogwood is particular about where it's planted, and if incorrectly sited, it's plagued by a host of pests and diseases. A fungus called dogwood anthracnose is the most serious and attacks stressed trees from coast to coast.

PAGODA DOGWOOD

Cornus alternifolia

Hardiness:
Zones 3–7

Shape:
Rounded

Color:
White flower, blue and red fruit, red-purple fall leaf

Texture:
Medium

Light:
Full sun to part shade

Size:
15–25 ft. high and wide

Character:
Medium deciduous tree grown for spring flower, red fall foliage, red and blue summer fruit

Named for its architectural branch structure, pagoda dogwood is a graceful, underrated, disease-resistant denizen of the eastern United States. A fast-growing small tree for gardens and patios, pagoda's fuzzy white spring flowers give way to striking blue fruit with a red stalk, and it's a favorite of birds.

CHINESE DOGWOOD

Cornus kousa

Hardiness:
Zones 5–8

Texture:
Medium

Shape:
Rounded

Light:
Full sun to part shade

Color:
White or pink flower, red fruit, red-purple fall leaf

Size:
15–30 ft. high and wide

Character:
Medium deciduous tree grown for white or pink spring flower; red summer fruit, red-purple fall foliage

Chinese dogwood is the disease-resistant Asian cousin of *Cornus florida*. It's a late bloomer, but takes center stage when it does. Flowers give way to red fruit birds love, and glossy leaves turn crimson and purple in fall. Cultivars are available for flower color from white to pink.

DOGWOOD

'MORNING CLOUD' CHITALPA

×Chitalpa tashkentensis 'Morning Cloud'

Hardiness:
Zones 6–11

Shape:
Open to rounded

Color:
Pink flower

Texture:
Medium

Light:
Full sun to part shade

Size:
20–35 ft. high and wide

Character:
Small deciduous tree grown for multiseason pink flower

A hybrid of two natives, catalpa (*Catalpa bignoniodes*) and desert willow (*Chilopsis linearis*), sun-loving chitalpa challenges any small tree for dry climates, boasting long summer bloom and a flair for the tropical. Chitalpa may mildew in the humid South, and pale pink-flowered 'Morning Cloud' resists mildew best.

● ● ● ● ● ● ● ● ● ● ● ● ● ● ● ● ● ●

ELM

Ulmus americana

Hardiness: **Zones 2–9**

Shape: **Vase to spreading**

Color: **Yellow fall leaf**

Texture: **Medium**

Light: **Full sun**

Size: **60–80 ft. high, 40–70 ft. wide**

Character:
Large deciduous tree grown for vase shape, size

As graceful, tree-lined boulevards came of age in the America of yesteryear, elm became their icon. The upperclassman all the other trees would look up to, this giant's claim to fame is its elegant vase-shaped trunk. In the 1930s, a devastating fungus called Dutch elm disease decimated native elm populations, and the species has been a fading beauty ever since.

HARDY RUBBER TREE

Eucommia ulmoides

Hardiness:
Zones 4–7

Shape:
Rounded to mounded

Color:
Yellow fall leaf

Texture:
Medium, glossy

Light:
Full sun to part shade

Size:
40–60 ft. high and wide

Character:
Small deciduous tree grown for mounded shape, glossy texture

Small enough in stature to find a home even in the most modest gardens, hardy rubber tree is disease-free, content in a wide range of soil types and conditions, and its glossy green leaves wink and glint enchantingly in the light. Its species name is *ulmoides* because of those leaves and their resemblance to the leaves of elm.

ELM

DISEASE-RESISTANT ELM

Ulmus americana 'Valley Forge'

Hardiness:
Zones (4)5–9

Shape:
Vase

Color:
Yellow fall leaf

Texture:
Medium

Light:
Full sun

Size:
60–70 ft. high, 50–60 ft. wide

Character:
Large deciduous tree grown for vase shape, size

In the face of disease, horticulturists took on the challenge of preserving American elm for future generations. Several disease-resistant cultivars emerged, and while no native elm is immune, 'Valley Forge' stands the best chance to survive and thrive. A fast-growing shade tree like its big brother, 'Valley Forge' has proven reliably cold-hardy up to Zone 5.

FLOSS SILK TREE

Ceiba speciosa

Hardiness:
Zones 9–11

Shape:
Vase to rounded, spreading

Color:
Pink or white flower, white fruit

Texture:
Bold in leaf, fine in flower and seed

Light:
Full sun

Size:
60–200 ft. high, 25–60 ft. wide

Character:
Large deciduous tree grown for pink fall flower, white winter fruit, size, ornamental trunk

A party girl year-round in warm climates, floss silk tree brings a spectacular flower show, drought tolerance, and adaptability, and it grows fast. Trained to a single trunk, it becomes umbrella-shaped with age. In fall, pink flowers appear, a prelude to poufy seedheads, and its thorny trunk is striking in winter.

61

HEMLOCK

Tsuga canadensis

🌡️	Hardiness:	**Zones 3–7**
🌲	Shape:	**Pyramidal**
🪶	Color:	**Green leaf, red-brown bark**
#	Texture:	**Fine, soft**
☼	Light:	**Part shade to full shade**
📏	Size:	**40–70 ft. high, 25–35 ft. wide**

Character:
Large evergreen tree grown for year-round foliage, pyramidal shape, fine texture

Hemlock is the grand dame of the temperate forest—*temperate* being the key word. This gentle giant much prefers cold climates, shade, and rich woodland soils. Sadly, a pest called woolly adelgid has decimated hemlock populations in its native range, and poorly planted trees sited in sun and droughty soils only serve to spread the pest.

EASTERN RED CEDAR

Juniperus virginiana

Hardiness:
Zones 2–9

Shape:
Oval to pyramidal

Color:
Green leaf, red-brown bark

Texture:
Fine, soft

Light:
Full sun

Size:
30–60 ft. high, 10–25 ft. wide

Character:
Small to medium evergreen tree grown for year-round foliage, pyramidal shape, fine texture

Underrated as a tough landscape tree, eastern red cedar grows fast, sneers at heat and drought, and provides food and shelter for wildlife as a native of thirty-seven U.S. states and Canada. This aromatic tree has yellow-green foliage and reddish, peeling bark, prefers sun, and adapts well to urban conditions and wet or dry soils.

DAWN REDWOOD

Metasequoia glyptostroboides

Hardiness:
Zones 4–8

Shape:
Pyramidal

Color:
**Green leaf,
orange fall leaf,
red-brown bark**

Texture:
Fine, soft

Light:
Full sun

Size:
**70–100 ft. high,
15–25 ft. wide**

Character:
**Large deciduous tree grown for
pyramidal shape, orange fall foliage,
fine texture, ornamental trunk**

Dawn redwood remains a unique beauty in
American gardens despite its availability,
ease of culture, classic silhouette, and delicate,
ferny foliage that turns to tones of rust and
soft orange in fall. Its fluted, cinnamon-colored
trunk makes a striking garden accent, and
as a deciduous tree, it's kinder to the smaller
kids in the schoolyard of the garden below.

63

HEMLOCK

JAPANESE UMBRELLA PINE

Sciadopitys verticillata

Hardiness:
Zones 5–8

Shape:
Pyramidal

Color:
Green leaf

Texture:
Fine, glossy

Light:
Full sun to part shade

Size:
25–30 ft. high, 15–20 ft. wide

Character:
Small to medium evergreen tree grown for year-round foliage, pyramidal shape, fine texture

Where a valedictorian of evergreens is called for, Japanese umbrella pine makes the grade. Looking for all the world like something from the age of the dinosaurs, umbrella pine excels in sun or part shade, in warm and cool climates, and with enough restraint for careful consideration even in small gardens.

64

ITALIAN CYPRESS

Cupressus sempervirens

🌡	Hardiness:	**Zones 7–10**
🌿	Shape:	**Columnar**
🍃	Color:	**Green leaf**
#	Texture:	**Fine, soft**
☼	Light:	**Full sun**
📏	Size:	**40–70 ft. high, 5–10 ft. wide**

Character:
Large evergreen tree grown for columnar shape, year-round foliage, fine texture

Summoning visions of Tuscan estates, Italian cypress is forever the haughty foreign exchange student, making a bold, outrageous vertical statement wherever it goes. This conifer's exclamatory form means it's challenging to mesh well into home gardens, and some see it as an eyesore. As a Mediterranean native, it gets the sniffles in cold, damp northern climes.

'DEGROOT'S SPIRE' ARBORVITAE

Thuja occidentalis 'Degroot's Spire'

Hardiness:
Zones 2–7

Shape:
Conical to columnar

Color:
Green leaf

Texture:
Fine, soft

Light:
Full sun to part shade

Size:
20–30 ft. high, 4–6 ft. wide

Character:
Small evergreen tree grown for columnar shape, year-round foliage, fine texture

'Degroot's Spire' arborvitae makes for a vertical accent that plays nice, even in cold-climate gardens, and since it's a slower-growing dwarf conifer, an all-star addition to small gardens as well. This *Thuja* is a cultivar of native white cedar (*T. occidentalis*) and offers great shelter for birds.

ITALIAN CYPRESS

'SHAWNEE BRAVE' BALDCYPRESS

Taxodium distichum 'Shawnee Brave'

Hardiness: **Zones 4–11**	Texture: **Fine, soft**
Shape: **Columnar to conical**	Light: **Full sun**
Color: **Green leaf, orange fall leaf**	Size: **50–75 ft. high, 15–20 ft. wide**

Character:
Large deciduous tree grown for columnar shape, orange fall foliage, fine texture

Another cultivar of a native plant, 'Shawnee Brave' baldcypress fits the bill for those in search of the tallest vertical accent, whether in wet soils or dry, hot or cold climates. Baldcypresses are the toughest kids on the schoolyard, and this one packs the punch of the species into a striking upright form.

INCENSE CEDAR

Calocedrus decurrens

Hardiness:
Zones 5–8

Shape:
Columnar to conical

Color:
Green leaf

Texture:
Fine, soft

Light:
Full sun to light shade

Size:
30–70 ft. high, 10–20 ft. wide

Character:
Small to medium evergreen tree grown for columnar shape, year-round foliage, fine texture

A western native tree, incense cedar thrives as far north as Zone 5, makes an elegant, dense column in the garden, and like white cedar (*Thuja occidentalis*), translates to terrific cover for birds. Needles smell of incense when crushed. This cedar takes dry soils well, but needs protection from drying winds.

● ● ● ● ● ● ● ● ● ● ● ● ● ● ● ● ● ● ●

JACARANDA

Jacaranda species

🌡	Hardiness:	**Zones 9–11**
🌲	Shape:	**Rounded to spreading**
🎨	Color:	**Blue-lavender flower**
#	Texture:	**Fine**
☀	Light:	**Full sun**
📏	Size:	**25–40 ft. high and wide**

Character:
Large deciduous tree grown for lavender spring and summer flower

A most memorable tropical tree, blooming jacaranda puts on the kind of show that stops the neighborhood in its tracks, with brilliant clumps of lavender-blue trumpets. If it were hardy beyond Zone 9, jacaranda could take the nation by storm, but this party girl will not grow in the cold.

REDBUD

Cercis canadensis

Hardiness:
Zones 4–9

Shape:
Rounded to spreading

Color:
Pink-lavender flower, gold fall leaf

Texture:
Fine in flower, bold in leaf

Light:
Full sun to part shade

Size:
20–30 ft. high, 25–35 ft. wide

Character:
Small deciduous tree grown for pink spring flower, gold fall foliage, and multiseason purple or gold foliage in cultivars

Zone 4–hardy redbud is the cover girl for top small garden trees. It blooms lavender-pink in spring, bears graceful heart-shaped leaves, grows well in part shade, and boasts terrific fall color. Cultivars for various traits exist, like purple-leaved 'Forest Pansy', gold-leaved 'Hearts of Gold', and drought-tolerant Texas redbud.

JACARANDA

'BLUE SATIN'
ROSE OF SHARON

Hibiscus syriacus 'Blue Satin'

Hardiness:
Zones 5–8

Shape:
Rounded

Color:
**Blue-lavender
flower, gold
fall leaf**

Texture:
Medium to bold

Light:
Full sun

Size:
**8–12 ft. high,
4–6 ft. wide**

Character:
**Small deciduous tree or large
shrub grown for blue-lavender
summer flower**

Rose of Sharon is a small tree familiar to
many gardeners, but this all-star cultivar is
guaranteed to wow with its sea of blue blooms
in mid- to late summer, a rarity among trees.
An easy, adaptable plant, 'Blue Satin' in
sun will tackle drought and bear flowers when
little else is in bloom. Most rose of Sharon
cultivars seed around in ideal conditions, so
watch for unwanted offspring.

TEXAS MOUNTAIN LAUREL

Calia secundiflora

Hardiness:
Zones 8–10

Shape:
**Rounded to
open, mounded**

Color:
**Blue to light
blue flower**

Texture:
**Medium to fine,
glossy**

Light:
**Full sun to
light shade**

Size:
**15–25 ft. high,
5–15 ft. wide**

Character:
**Small evergreen tree grown for
fragrant blue summer flower; year-
round foliage, mounded shape**

For all the flower power in an evergreen,
Texas mountain laurel packs a springtime
punch when it blooms brilliantly blue, and
with fruit punch fragrance to boot. This
droughty beauty grows slowly and makes an
ideal small patio tree north to Zone 8. It is
sometimes sold as *Sophora secundiflora*.

71

JAPANESE MAPLE

Acer palmatum and cultivars

🌡	Hardiness:	**Zones 5–9**
🌲	Shape:	**Vase to rounded**
🖌	Color:	**Green, red, or gold leaf; variable fall color**
⊞	Texture:	**Fine to medium**
☼	Light:	**Light shade to full shade**
📏	Size:	**10–25 ft. high and wide**

Character:
Small deciduous tree grown for fine texture, multiseason foliage in various colors in cultivars, fall foliage in various colors

The prom queen of plants for the Japanese-style garden, Japanese maple is a small tree that bestows a colorful laciness on shady gardens in soils of average moisture. All of its many cultivars much prefer not to live in hot sun, dry or extremely cold climates.

ELDERBERRY

Sambucus species and cultivars

Hardiness:
Zones 3–9

Shape:
Vase

Color:
Purple, gold, or green leaf

Texture:
Fine to medium

Light:
Full sun to part shade

Size:
15–25 ft. high, 10 ft. wide

Character:
Small deciduous tree grown for fine texture, multiseason purple or gold foliage in cultivars, edible summer fruit

Hardy and hearty, elderberry thrives in a range of climates, light, and soils. Colorful cultivars 'Black Lace' (pictured) and 'Sutherland Gold' handle drier soils and more sun. Native *Sambucus canadensis* dislikes drought, but it's beloved for berries by bird and human. Elders benefit from some shade in the heat of the day.

PAPERBARK MAPLE

Acer griseum

Hardiness:
Zones 4–8

Shape:
Vase to rounded

Color:
Green leaf, red-orange bark, red fall leaf

Texture:
Fine, glossy

Light:
Full sun to part shade

Size:
20–30 ft. high, 15–25 ft. wide

Character:
Small deciduous tree grown for fine texture, red bark year-round, fine texture, red fall foliage

Paperbark maple isn't just an underused star a whole zone colder than Japanese maple, it's more versatile too. In sun or shade, its peeling, reddish-brown bark is gorgeous backed by winter snow or a midsummer sunset. It can be a slow grower, so better to invest in a bigger plant up front.

73

JAPANESE MAPLE

VINE MAPLE

Acer circinatum

Hardiness:
Zones 6–9

Shape:
Vase to rounded

Color:
Green leaf, red, gold, and orange fall leaf

Texture:
Fine to medium

Light:
Light shade to full shade

Size:
20–30 ft. high and wide

Character:
Small deciduous tree grown for fine texture, fall foliage in various colors

The Pacific Northwest lays claim to vine maple, a Western version of the Japanese tree all its own. Where it's native, vine maple brings value-added versatility of food and shelter for birds and mammals of all kind, and adapts better to drought in temperate climates than its Japanese cousin to boot.

LIVE OAK

Quercus virginiana

🌡	Hardiness:	**Zones 8–10**
🌳	Shape:	**Open, rounded to spreading**
🖌	Color:	**Green leaf**
#	Texture:	**Medium to fine**
☀	Light:	**Full sun**
📏	Size:	**40–80 ft. tall, 60–100 ft. wide**

Character:
Large evergreen tree grown for spreading shape, size

Southern live oak could be characterized as "Most Venerable Old Professor" at the garden school. Its breadth is best appreciated standing beneath its massive, rambling crown; huge, gnarled limbs may almost reach the ground. Like that old professor, it can be a little messy, and it's not a fan of cold—you won't grow it far north of Zone 8.

BUR OAK

Quercus macrocarpa

Hardiness:
Zones 3–9

Shape:
Open, rounded to spreading

Color:
Green leaf

Texture:
Medium to bold, glossy

Light:
Full sun

Size:
35–80 ft. high and wide

Character:
Medium to large deciduous tree grown for spreading shape, size

Bur oak brings big personality to any space. This towering, hardy tree is a multitalented native from the Great Plains to the Northeast. Its name comes from its scaly acorns, adored by wildlife, and it adapts to many soils and situations. Bur oak shows great drought tolerance and makes less of a mess than many of the oak clan.

LIVE OAK

EUROPEAN BEECH

Fagus sylvatica and cultivars

Hardiness:
Zones 4–7

Texture:
Medium, glossy

Shape:
Oval to rounded

Light:
Full sun

Color:
Green or purple leaf in cultivars, red to gold fall leaf

Size:
50–75 ft. high, 40–60 ft. wide

Character:
Large deciduous tree grown for size, purple leaf in cultivars, gold fall foliage

European beech is top of its class in northern climates. Its huge, shimmering crown above matches a smooth, elephant-gray trunk below. Left unpruned, its lower limbs gracefully brush the ground. Many common purple-leaved cultivars, called copper beech, make supersized color accents where space permits. Leaves turn to red and gold in fall.

KATSURA

Cercidiphyllum japonicum

Hardiness: **Zones 4–8**	**Character:** **Medium to large deciduous tree grown for spreading shape, fragrant gold fall foliage**
Shape: **Rounded, spreading in old age**	
Color: **Blue-green leaf, gold fall leaf**	It's impossible not to love katsura, a cold-hardy tree with excellent form and gorgeous autumn color from leaves that smell of cinnamon when they fall. Rounded in youth, katsura spreads out at maturity, its stout trunk and shallow, knotted surface roots ornamental in themselves. Katsura tolerates drought at maturity as well.
Texture: **Medium, soft**	
Light: **Full sun to part shade**	
Size: **40–60 ft. high, 25–60 ft. wide**	

● ● ● ● ● ● ● ● ● ● ● ● ● ● ● ● ●

LOMBARDY POPLAR

Populus nigra 'Italica'

🌡	Hardiness:	**Zones 4–9**
🌿	Shape:	**Columnar**
🖌	Color:	**Gold fall leaf**
#	Texture:	**Medium**
☀	Light:	**Full sun**
📏	Size:	**60 ft. high, 10 ft. wide**

Character:
Small deciduous tree grown for columnar shape

Growing straight as an arrow upwards of 60 feet, Lombardy poplar is a messy troublemaker with meddling, fast-growing roots. Its penchant for canker disease means it rarely reaches its full potential and quickly becomes a garden dropout, an eyesore, and a liability.

'FASTIGIATA' HORNBEAM

Carpinus betulus 'Fastigiata'

🌡 🌿 🖌 # ☀ 📏

Hardiness:
Zones 4–8

Shape:
Columnar to oval, mounded

Color:
Gold to orange fall leaf

Texture:
Medium, glossy

Light:
Full sun to part shade

Size:
30–40 ft. high, 20–30 ft. wide

Character:
Small deciduous tree grown for columnar shape, mounded shape, as hedge

In botany, *fastigiate* means upright, and 'Fastigiata' hornbeam is the model student. Unbothered by disease, this dense, narrow tree bears handsome fall foliage and exquisite gray bark. Hornbeam shines as a street or lawn tree and can even be sheared into a hedge.

'SLENDER SILHOUETTE' SWEET GUM

Liquidambar styraciflua 'Slender Silhouette'

Hardiness: **Zones 5–9**	Texture: **Medium, glossy**
Shape: **Columnar**	Light: **Full sun to part shade**
Color: **Orange, gold, and red fall leaf**	Size: **50 ft. high, 6 ft. wide**

Character:
Small deciduous tree grown for columnar shape, fall foliage in various colors

A cultivar of eastern native sweet gum, 'Slender Silhouette' not only makes a disease-free vertical accent in the garden, it also sets the curve with outstanding gold to burgundy fall foliage. 'Slender Silhouette' produces fewer spiky fruits than sweet gum is known for and works fantastically in small gardens.

LOMBARDY POPLAR

TREE CACTI

Various species

Hardiness:
Zones 8b–10

Shape:
Columnar

Color:
Bluish green to gold stems, variable flower color

Texture:
Bold

Light:
Full sun

Size:
20 ft. or more high, 1–2 ft. wide

Character:
Large evergreen succulent grown for columnar shape, flower in various seasons and colors

The most famously vertical plants of all, tree cacti are at the top of their class for gardeners in dry, mostly frost-free climates. Saguaro (*Carnegiea gigantea*) is pricey, but fencepost cacti (*Pachycereus marginatus* and *Echinopsis pachanoi*, pictured) are affordable and easy to find. Hardier is cone cactus (*Neobuxbaumia polylopha*), to Zone 8b. All grow slowly, easily, and make the best of vertical accents in tight spaces.

● ● ● ● ● ● ● ● ● ● ● ● ● ● ● ● ● ● ●

MAGNOLIA

Magnolia grandiflora

	Hardiness:	**Zones (6)7–10**
	Shape:	**Pyramidal to rounded**
	Color:	**White flower, red fruit**
	Texture:	**Bold, glossy**
	Light:	**Full sun to part shade**
	Size:	**60–80 ft. high, 30–50 ft. wide**

Character:
Large evergreen tree grown for fragrant white summer flower, bold texture, year-round foliage, size

The pop icon of southern flowering trees, southern magnolia will not be ignored. Towering and glossy-leaved, with huge, fragrant flowers, it's fairly hardy, but breaks under heavy snow up north. This magnolia constantly showers its surroundings with litter, and its impenetrable canopy and root system make it a difficult garden companion anywhere.

CUCUMBER MAGNOLIA

Magnolia acuminata and cultivars

Hardiness:
Zones 3–8

Shape:
Pyramidal

Color:
Yellow-green flower, gold fall leaf

Texture:
Bold

Light:
Full sun to part shade

Size:
40–70 ft. high, 20–35 ft. wide

Character:
Large deciduous tree grown for size, bold texture, yellow spring flower, yellow fall foliage

Eastern native cucumber magnolia puts up with snow, its canopy is kinder to plants below, its flower pale yellow and fall foliage gold. It's similar in size and form to southern magnolia, but for smaller spaces, *Magnolia acuminata* 'Koban Dori' and hybrids *M.* 'Elizabeth' and *M.* 'Butterflies' fit in stature and are fancier in flower.

MAGNOLIA

SWEET BAY MAGNOLIA

Magnolia virginiana

Hardiness:
Zones 5–10

Shape:
Rounded

Color:
White flower, red fruit

Texture:
Medium to bold, glossy

Light:
Full sun to part shade

Size:
10–35 ft. high and wide

Character:
Small evergreen tree grown for year-round foliage, fragrant white summer flower, red fall fruit

Hardy in a huge range across the continent, sweet bay magnolia is a shy student who nonetheless graces the garden with lemon-scented flowers, red fruit, and glossy leaves that are evergreen in warmer climates. Unlike its cousins, it adores wet soils, though average sites are fine too.

OYAMA MAGNOLIA

Magnolia sieboldii

Hardiness: **Zones 6–9**	Texture: **Bold**
Shape: **Upright to rounded**	Light: **Full sun to part shade**
Color: **White, red, and yellow flower, gold fall leaf**	Size: **15–30 ft. high and wide**

Character:
**Small deciduous tree grown for
fragrant white flower, bold texture**

For hardiness and flower power, Oyama magnolia can't be beat. Fragrant white flowers look like eggs to start out and open to reveal red-pink and yellow centers. Big, blousy leaves are a treat throughout the season. Cultivars like 'Colossus' make even bigger flowers (to 5 inches in diameter) and leaves (to 18 inches long).

83

MIMOSA

Albizia julibrissin

🌡	Hardiness:	**Zones 6–9**
🌲	Shape:	**Spreading**
🌸	Color:	**Pink flower**
▦	Texture:	**Fine, soft**
☼	Light:	**Full sun to part shade**
📏	Size:	**20–40 ft. high, 20–50 ft. wide**

Character:
Small to medium deciduous tree grown for fragrant pink spring flower, fine texture

Exotic beauty mimosa suggests a breath of the tropics, as well as the Far East. It's also a brazen hussy, spreading its seedlings across the U.S. Southeast. Lacey leaves complement distinctive puffy pink flowers, pretty until they brown and make a mess.

HONEYLOCUST

Gleditsia triacanthos var. *inermis* cultivars

Hardiness:
Zones 3–9

Shape:
Open, spreading

Color:
Gold fall leaf

Texture:
Fine, glossy

Light:
Full sun to light shade

Size:
40–50 ft. high, 30–40 ft. wide

Character:
Medium to large deciduous tree grown for fine texture, gold fall foliage

Native honeylocust is a linebacker among trees. A beacon of fall gold adaptable to almost any climate and design, honeylocust meshes into garden styles from tropical to Mediterranean, sidewalk to savannah. Thornless, seedless varieties mean little mess, and their open canopies mean it's easier to garden under these trees.

YELLOWWOOD

Cladrastis kentukea

Hardiness:
Zones 4–8

Texture:
Medium

Shape:
Rounded to spreading

Light:
Full sun

Color:
White flower, pink flower in cultivar, gold fall leaf

Size:
60–80 ft. high, 40–50 ft. wide

Character:
Small to medium deciduous tree grown for fragrant white or pink spring flower, gold fall foliage

It goes by yellowwood, but this small tree strikes it rich with gold fall leaves and either white spring bloom in the species or pink in the cultivar 'Rosea'—a feast in sight and scent. A Southeast native, yellowwood is also cold-hardy as far north as Zone 4.

85

MIMOSA

RED BIRD-OF-PARADISE

Caesalpinia pulcherimma

Hardiness:
Zones (8)9–11

Shape:
Spreading

Color:
Bluish leaf, red-orange flower

Texture:
Fine, soft

Light:
Full sun to part shade

Size:
18–20 ft. high and wide

Character:
Large deciduous shrub or small tree grown for red-orange summer flower, fine texture, multiseason blue foliage

Red bird-of-paradise is a punk making a bold statement in hot climates, dry and humid, where mimosa makes trouble. Red-orange in flower and bluish in leaf, this flamboyant bird is better for small spaces, especially in Zones 8–9a, where it can be grown as a large shrub and cut to the ground in winter.

NORWAY MAPLE

Acer platanoides and cultivars

🌡	Hardiness:	**Zones 3–7**
🌲	Shape:	**Rounded**
🔌	Color:	**Green or purple leaf, yellow fall leaf**
▦	Texture:	**Medium**
☀	Light:	**Full sun to part shade**
📐	Size:	**40–50 ft. high, 30–50 ft. wide**

Character:
Large deciduous tree grown for size, multiseason purple foliage in cultivar

Invasive Norway maple is a school bully, trouncing native ecosystems in much of its American growing range with impenetrable canopy above and root system below. Its fall color is mediocre, and outside its preferred climate it struggles in high heat and humidity. Maroon cultivar 'Crimson King' is equally rude, casting seeds to the wind that revert to the species.

SUGAR MAPLE

Acer saccharum

Hardiness:
Zones 3–8

Shape:
Rounded

Color:
Green leaf, yellow to gold to orange fall leaf

Texture:
Medium

Light:
Full sun to part shade

Size:
40–80 ft. high, 30–60 ft. wide

Character:
Large deciduous tree grown for size, fall foliage in various colors

Sugar maple is a treasured American mascot. In autumn forests of the East, it dazzles in oranges and golds, and like all native maples, it benefits countless species of wildlife all year. For people, it yields not only good shade, but also liquid tradition in the form of maple syrup. Plant sugar maple where its roots can spread out, as it doesn't like compacted soil.

NORWAY MAPLE

RED MAPLE

Acer rubrum

Hardiness:
Zones 3–9

Shape:
Rounded

Color:
Green leaf, red flower, red fall leaf

Texture:
Medium

Light:
Full sun to part shade

Size:
40–70 ft. high, 30–50 ft. wide

Character:
Medium to large deciduous tree grown for red fall foliage

Happy with wet feet or dry, adaptable red maple bursts into a fiery display in fall and again in spring, when it blooms. Red maple thrives in average soils but grows naturally in wetlands, so it's ideal for rain gardens and soils that get periodically soaked. Like sugar maple, it's key in its native ecosystem. Plant maples away from walks and driveways—their shallow roots may disturb pavement.

BIGLEAF MAPLE

Acer macrophyllum

Hardiness:
Zones 6–9

Shape:
Rounded

Color:
**Green leaf, gold
to orange fall leaf**

Texture:
Medium to bold

Light:
**Full sun to
part shade**

Size:
**40–70 ft. high,
30–60 ft. wide**

Character:
**Medium to large deciduous tree
grown for size, bold texture, fall
foliage in various colors**

A chilly customer native to cooler sites the
length of the West Coast, bigleaf maple grows
tall and fast, adapts well to dry sites in its
home range, and like its eastern cousins, is
invaluable to wildlife. Bigleaf maple's leaves
aren't just big, they're the biggest of any
maple, some over a foot across.

89

OLIVE

Olea europaea

🌡	Hardiness:	**Zones 8–10**
🌲	Shape:	**Spreading**
🍃	Color:	**Silver leaf**
▦	Texture:	**Fine to medium, soft**
☀	Light:	**Full sun**
✂	Size:	**20–30 ft. tall, 15–20 ft. wide**

Character:
Small evergreen tree or large shrub grown for edible fall fruit, year-round silver foliage

Known first for fruit, second for beauty, olive evokes wild elegance—its silvery leaves a shimmering garden accent—and gnarled trunks exude faded grace. Olive is the exciting substitute teacher you wish could stick around, but alas, it's a Mediterranean plant, and its tenure in all but warm, dry climates will be short.

ROSEMARY WILLOW

Salix elaeagnos

Hardiness:
Zones 4–7

Shape:
Rounded

Color:
Silver leaf

Texture:
Fine, soft

Light:
Full sun to part shade

Size:
10–12 ft. tall and wide

Character:
Small deciduous tree or large shrub grown for multiseason silver foliage

Little known rosemary willow is cold-hardy, silver-leaved, and thrives in gardens big and small. Like lots of little willows, it can be cut to the ground and allowed to regrow as a shrub each spring, or trained easily to be a big tree. Its eye-catching foliage illuminates any corner where it's planted.

GOUMI

Elaeagnus multiflora

Hardiness:
Zones 4–9

Texture:
Medium, soft

Shape:
Rounded

Light:
Full sun to part shade

Color:
Silver leaf, red fruit

Size:
8–10 ft. high and wide

Character:
Large deciduous shrub or small tree grown for edible summer fruit, fragrant yellow spring flower, multiseason silver foliage

Fragrant, pale yellow flowers adorn goumi in spring, followed by silver-speckled leaves and tart red berries. Shrubby and drought tolerant, goumi shines in sun or part shade and all but the wettest soils. Fruit falls when it's ripe and works well in pies and jellies.

OLIVE

PINEAPPLE GUAVA

Acca sellowiana

Hardiness: **Zones (7)8–11**	Texture: **Medium, soft**
Shape: **Upright, mounded**	Light: **Full sun to part shade**
Color: **Pink flower, silver leaf**	Size: **10–15 ft. high and wide**

Character:
Large evergreen shrub grown for pink spring flower, edible summer fruit, year-round silver foliage, mounded shape, as hedge

For a knockout combination of flower and foliage, look no further than pineapple guava. Its silvery leaves are a sign of drought tolerance, but the plant does great in humid climates too. Guava blooms in spring, each flower an array of red stamens cloaked in pink petals. Flowers are edible, as are sporadic fruits. Pineapple guava is often found for sale as *Feijoa sellowiana*.

93

ORNAMENTAL FRUIT TREES

Malus cultivars / *Prunus* cultivars

	Hardiness:	**Zones 4–9**
	Shape:	**Open, rounded, spreading or weeping**
	Color:	**Pink, red, or white flower**
	Texture:	**Medium**
	Light:	**Full sun to light shade**
	Size:	**15–25 ft. high and wide**

Character:
Small deciduous tree grown for spring flower in various colors

Debutantes of a once-a-year ball, ornamental crabapple, cherry, and plum trees bloom flirtatiously in spring and segue into mediocrity the rest of the year. These trees need frequent pruning to be at their best and make common targets for pests and diseases.
In crabapple's case, messy fruit is yet another reason to steer clear.

'ROBIN HILL' SHADBLOW

Amelanchier ×grandiflora 'Robin Hill'

Hardiness:
Zones 4–9

Shape:
Oval to rounded

Color:
Pink flower, gold to red fall leaf

Texture:
Medium

Light:
Full sun to part shade

Size:
15–25 ft. high and wide

Character:
Small deciduous tree grown for pink spring flower, summer fruit, fall foliage in various colors

A multiseason heartbreaker, this small tree is a hybrid of two eastern natives (*Amelanchier arborea* and *A. laevis*). Unlike its white-flowered parents, 'Robin Hill' shadblow blooms in pale pink in spring, followed by edible berries, and finishes up with outstanding red to gold fall foliage.

CHINESE FRINGE TREE

Chionanthus retusus

Hardiness:	Texture:
Zones 5–9	**Medium, glossy**

Shape:	Light:
Spreading	**Full sun to part shade**

Color:	
White flower, gold fall leaf	

	Size:
	10–20 ft. high and wide

Character:
Small deciduous tree grown for white spring flower, gold fall foliage, blue fall fruit

A sweeping cloudscape of fragrant white flowers in spring, Chinese fringe tree follows bloom with brilliant foliage that turns gold in fall, when female plants produce blue berries. Tough and adaptable to street or patio, it's rarely bothered by diseases and pests, and needs little pruning.

95

ORNAMENTAL FRUIT TREES

'PURPUREA' ACACIA

Acacia baileyana 'Purpurea'

Hardiness:
Zones 9–11

Shape:
Spreading

Color:
Purple leaf, gold flower

Texture:
Fine to medium, soft

Light:
Full sun

Size:
20–30 ft. high and wide

Character:
Small evergreen tree grown for year-round purple foliage, fragrant yellow spring flower

A dazzlingly multifaceted small tree for Zones 9 and higher, purple-leaved acacia grows fast, thrives in heat and drought, sports fragrant yellow flowers from winter to spring, and new foliage in a deep, soft purple year-round. Leaves age to steely blue. Pruning promotes additional purple growth.

WEEPING WILLOW

Salix alba and cultivars / *Salix babylonica*

🌡	Hardiness:	**Zones 2–9**
☁	Shape:	**Weeping**
🔌	Color:	**Green leaf**
#	Texture:	**Fine, glossy**
☼	Light:	**Full sun to part shade**
📏	Size:	**50–80 ft. high, 40–70 ft. wide**

Character:
Large deciduous tree grown for weeping shape, fine texture

A pillar of elegance, weeping willow easily wins "Most Popular Weeping Tree." Ironically, it's like a messy teen that feathers its nest with leaf litter, limbs prone to breaking, and brings home all the bugs from school. Like many willows, its roots seek water and may play havoc with utilities.

WEEPING KATSURA

Cercidiphyllum japonicum 'Pendula' / *Cercidiphyllum japonicum* 'Morioka Weeping'

Hardiness:
Zones 4–8

Shape:
Weeping, irregular

Color:
Blue-green leaf, gold fall leaf

Texture:
Medium, soft

Light:
Full sun to part shade

Size:
15–25 ft. high, 10–15 ft. wide

Character:
Small deciduous tree grown for weeping shape, fragrant gold fall foliage

Weeping katsura boasts waterfalls of bluish leaves that warm to gold in autumn and smell of cinnamon as they fall. Its modest stature means it works for small gardens, yet its presence is substantial. 'Morioka Weeping' is the sturdier of the two weeping cultivars, though 'Pendula' (pictured) isn't far behind.

WEEPING WILLOW

RIVER BIRCH

Betula nigra 'Heritage'

Hardiness:
Zones 4–9

Shape:
Weeping, pyramidal to rounded

Color:
Green leaf, red-brown bark

Texture:
Medium to fine, glossy

Light:
Full sun to part shade

Size:
50–70 ft. high, 40–60 ft. wide

Character:
Small to medium deciduous tree grown for red-brown bark, weeping shape, fine texture

River birch may be famed for multicolored, peeling bark, but this eastern native proves equally elegant for its pendulous form. This birch likes it damp, but adapts to soils of average moisture, and takes to heat and humidity better than others. The cultivar 'Heritage' resists disease best.

AUSTRALIAN WILLOW

Geijera parviflora

Hardiness: **Zones 9–11**	Texture: **Fine, soft**
Shape: **Weeping, oval to rounded**	Light: **Full sun to light shade**
Color: **Green leaf**	Size: **30–40 ft. high, 20 ft. wide**

Character:
Small to medium deciduous tree grown for weeping shape, fine texture, year-round foliage

A willow in name only, this all-star's delicate leaves cloak a sturdy structure. It blooms spring and fall with showy white flowers, stands up to the elements, and adapts to dry and wet soils. A tidy tree in any setting, Australian willow works well for patio, street, or lawn.

●●●●●●●●●●●●●●●●●●

Why be a plain green palm when you could
be variegated aralia (*Aralia elata* 'Variegata')?

100

Shrubs

If trees are the garden's big guns, shrubs are the popular, cool kids. Why? While trees reach for the sky, shrubs show off at eye level, and they're often the garden's biggest attention-getters—only some may need too much attention. Shrub troublemakers include some of the most high-maintenance prima donnas in the plant world. As with trees, if you choose the right shrubs, they make for garden goodness year-round. If you have a shrub you suspect may be a fallen star, follow along to learn about all-stars that are better alternatives.

ARBORVITAE

Thuja occidentalis

🌡	Hardiness:	**Zones 2–7**
🌲	Shape:	**Conical**
🍃	Color:	**Green leaf**
▦	Texture:	**Fine, soft**
☼	Light:	**Full sun to light shade**
📏	Size:	**20–40 ft. high, 10–15 ft. wide; typically pruned smaller**

Character:

Large evergreen shrub or small tree grown for year-round foliage, as hedge, fine texture

Arborvitae wants to be a star student, just not in the subjects you may hope. In nature, it's a tree. In home landscapes, it and common cultivars suffer, often badly sheared into hedges, or planted in sites too exposed or too shady. Arborvitae also founders in high-humidity climates.

ROCKY MOUNTAIN JUNIPER

Juniperus scopulorum 'Skyrocket' / *Juniperus scopulorum* 'Wichita Blue'

🌡 🌲 🍃 ▦ ☼ 📏

Hardiness:	**Zones 3–7**
Shape:	**Conical**
Color:	**Blue leaf**
Texture:	**Fine, soft**
Light:	**Full sun**
Size:	**10–15 ft. high, 4–6 ft. wide**

Character:

Large evergreen shrub or small tree grown for year-round blue foliage, as hedge, conical shape, fine texture

Rocky Mountain juniper grows wild in the mountains of the West. Cultivars 'Skyrocket' and 'Wichita Blue' (pictured) make excellent low-water screening for dry western zones and need little pruning or maintenance. Both have blue foliage, a year-round bonus, and excel in difficult sites.

'GREEN GIANT' ARBORVITAE

Thuja 'Green Giant'

Hardiness:
Zones 5–8

Shape:
Conical

Color:
Green leaf

Texture:
Fine, soft

Light:
Full sun to part shade

Size:
20–60 ft. high, 10–20 ft. wide

Character:
Large evergreen shrub or small tree grown for year-round foliage, as hedge, conical shape, fine texture

A hybrid of western red cedar (*Thuja plicata*) and Japanese arborvitae (*Thuja standishii*), 'Green Giant' shines as a garden plant. This selection adapts well to part shade and grows fast, making excellent, dense screening, and it's more amenable to shearing as a hedge. If left unpruned, it grows into a stately pyramidal tree.

ARBORVITAE

YAUPON

Ilex vomitoria and cultivars

Hardiness:
Zones 7–9

Texture:
Fine, glossy

Shape:
Mounded, upright to rounded

Light:
Full sun to part shade

Color:
Green leaf, red fruit

Size:
10–20 ft. high, 10–12 ft. wide

Character:
Large deciduous shrub or small tree grown for year-round foliage, as hedge, red fall fruit, fine texture

A native of the hot, humid Southeast, yaupon wins "Best All-Around" for sites of all kinds— from sunny and dry to shady and wet. Various cultivars work well as tall screen or short hedge, and provide valuable fruit and cover for birds. Male and female plants are a must for berries.

BARBERRY

Berberis thunbergii cultivars /
Berberis vulgaris cultivars

🌡	Hardiness:	**Zones 4–10**
🌿	Shape:	**Rounded, mounded**
🔌	Color:	**Red, purple, or gold fall leaf**
▦	Texture:	**Fine**
☼	Light:	**Full sun to part shade**
📏	Size:	**3–6 ft. high, 4–7 ft. wide**

Character:

Medium deciduous shrub grown for multiseason foliage in various colors, as hedge

A popular plant for red, purple, or gold foliage, prickly barberry is a troublemaking thug with a history—weedy since the early 1900s. It sets seed, reverts to green, and threatens to smother ecosystems from the Northeast to the Carolinas, west to Missouri. Where it isn't invasive, barberry is often overused.

NINEBARK

Physocarpus opulifolius cultivars

Hardiness:
Zones 2–8

Shape:
Upright, rounded to spreading, mounded

Color:
Red or gold leaf

Texture:
Medium

Light:
Full sun to part shade

Size:
4–8 ft. high and wide

Character:

Medium to large deciduous shrub grown for multiseason foliage in various colors

Ninebark cultivars dazzle in red, orange, purple, and gold, sometimes all in one plant, and this native also boasts berries for birds. Orange 'Coppertina' (pictured), purple 'Diabolo', and yellow 'Dart's Gold' are stars of the garden show, while red-purple 'Summer Wine' grows half the size. Fast-growing ninebark thrives in a range of conditions.

BARBERRY

'BAGGESEN'S GOLD' BOX HONEYSUCKLE

Lonicera nitida 'Baggesen's Gold'

Hardiness:	Texture:	Character:
Zones (4)5–9	**Fine**	**Small to medium semideciduous shrub grown for multiseason gold foliage, as hedge, as groundcover**
Shape:	Light:	
Mounded to spreading	**Light shade to part shade**	
Color:	Size:	
Gold leaf	**5 ft. high and wide**	

Compact, clean, and gleaming in shade, golden box honeysuckle looks good clipped into a hedge or left to grow on its own. This drought-tolerant beauty is semideciduous in cold climates, evergreen in mild. Its modest stature and natural manageability make it a great accent for small gardens.

'BRONZE BUTTERFLY' SHRUB

Gastrolobium praemorsum 'Bronze Butterfly'

Hardiness:	Texture:
Zones 9–11	**Fine**

Shape:	Light:
Rounded, mounded	**Full sun**

Color:	Size:
Red leaf	**1–2 ft. high, 3–4 ft. wide**

Character:
Small evergreen shrub grown for year-round red foliage, as hedge, as groundcover

Big bonbons of chocolaty red-purple describe this drought-tolerant little plant, great for small gardens and as a shrub and ground-cover. The pairs of tiny leaves are like butterflies along the red stems, and each leaf is edged in subtle, contrasting chartreuse—a stunning color combo. This plant is often sold as *Brachysema praemorsum* 'Bronze Butterfly'.

BOXWOOD

Buxus species and cultivars

🌡	Hardiness:	**Zones 4–9**
🌲	Shape:	**Mounded**
🍃	Color:	**Green leaf**
#	Texture:	**Fine, glossy**
☀	Light:	**Full sun to part shade**
✂	Size:	**5–8 ft. high, 10–15 ft. wide; typically pruned smaller**

Character:
Small to medium evergreen shrub grown for year-round foliage, as hedge, fine texture

Boxwood's popularity as a classic English garden hedge earns it a spot in many a garden where it's doomed to be a problem child—especially the hottest, driest, and most humid. Box thrives in cool climates with regular water, good drainage and air circulation. Outside its comfort zone, it almost inevitably invites pests and problems.

INKBERRY

Ilex glabra cultivars

Hardiness:
Zones 4–9

Shape:
Rounded, mounded

Color:
Green leaf, black fruit

Texture:
Fine to medium, glossy

Light:
Full sun to part shade

Size:
5–8 ft. high and wide

Character:
Small to medium evergreen shrub grown for year-round foliage, as hedge, black fall fruit

A versatile native from Nova Scotia to Florida, inkberry's compact cultivars make for a great hedge, adapting to wet soils and seaside conditions, sun or shade. Among the brightest stars are 'Compacta', 'Densa', and 'Shamrock'. Birds eat inkberry's black fruit, and bees go wild for its tiny flowers. Plant both male and female shrubs for fruit.

BOXWOOD

BAPTISIA

Baptisia species and cultivars

Hardiness: **Zones 3–9**	Texture: **Medium to fine**
Shape: **Rounded, mounded**	Light: **Full sun to part shade**
Color: **Blue-green leaf, red, orange, yellow, blue, purple, or white flower**	Size: **3–4 ft. high and wide**

Character:
Large herbaceous perennial grown for spring flower in various colors

Where soil is too shabby for shrubbery, baptisia and cultivars marvel as loose hedge during the growing season. Low-water native baptisia thrives on poor sites, and different varieties flower in blue, gold, purple, or white. Dwarf cultivars bedazzle small gardens.

TEXAS RANGER

Leucophyllum langmaniae cultivars

Hardiness:
Zones 7–10

Shape:
**Rounded,
mounded**

Color:
**Green leaf, pink
or purple flower**

Texture:
Fine, soft

Light:
**Full sun to
part shade**

Size:
**3–5 ft. high
and wide**

Character:
**Medium evergreen shrub grown for
year-round foliage, pink or purple
summer flower, as hedge, fine texture,
as groundcover**

Unlike its more familiar silver cousins
(*Leucophyllum frutescens* and cultivars), this
Texas Ranger species has small leaves of
green. It too makes excellent hedging in the
driest of gardens, and as an added bonus,
also thrives in part shade. Cultivars include
'Rio Bravo' (pictured) and 'Lynn's Legacy'.
Both bloom in lavender.

BURNING BUSH

Euonymus alatus

🌡	Hardiness:	**Zones 4–8**
🌳	Shape:	**Rounded**
🍃	Color:	**Red fall leaf**
▦	Texture:	**Medium**
☼	Light:	**Full sun to full shade**
📏	Size:	**8–20 ft. high, 8–12 ft. wide**

Character:
Large deciduous shrub or small tree grown for red fall foliage, as hedge

It's all fun and games until someone loses an ecosystem. Burning bush is the class clown of fall, a fire engine of foliage that sets the garden alight. It's also an invasive species with an evil root system, smothering forest floors across the East and Midwest, its seed scattered by unwitting birds.

EASTERN WAHOO

Euonymus atropurpureus

Hardiness: **Zones 3–7**	Texture: **Medium**
Shape: **Rounded to pyramidal, irregular**	Light: **Full sun to full shade**
Color: **Red fall leaf**	Size: **8–20 ft. high, 10–25 ft. wide**

Character:
Large deciduous shrub or small tree grown for red fall fruit and foliage

An American relative of *Euonymus alatus*, eastern wahoo boasts brilliant red fall leaves and dangly red berries, a treat both for birds and people. Wahoo adapts to a range of conditions and grows naturally over nearly half of North America.

HIGHBUSH BLUEBERRY/ RABBITEYE BLUEBERRY

BURNING BUSH

Vaccinium corymbosum cultivars
Vaccinium ashei cultivars

Hardiness:
Zones 3–9

Texture:
Medium, glossy

Shape:
Rounded, spreading

Light:
Full sun to part shade

Color:
Red to orange fall leaf

Size:
6–12 ft. high and wide

Character:
Large deciduous shrub grown for edible blue summer fruit

One of America's greatest native food plants may be its most underrated ornamental. Blueberry asks only average to moist, acidic soil. In return, it makes a glittery, glossy informal hedge, a fabulous red-purple in fall, and cultivars for any size garden. Highbush (pictured) needs cold zones; rabbiteye likes it warm.

FRAGRANT SUMAC

Rhus aromatica

Hardiness:
Zones 4–9

Shape:
**Rounded,
spreading**

Color:
**Red to orange
fall leaf**

Texture:
Medium, glossy

Light:
**Full sun to
part shade**

Size:
**2–6 ft. high,
6–10 ft. wide**

Character:
**Medium deciduous shrub grown for
red fall foliage**

For more fall red in a native, fragrant sumac
can't be beat. A stalwart plant as happy in
Arizona as Alabama, this low-water shrub
blooms too, with dainty cream clusters in
spring. Female plants produce velvety, bird-
friendly red berries in late summer.

● ● ● ● ● ● ● ● ● ● ● ● ● ● ● ● ●

CAMELLIA

Camellia japonica cultivars

🌡	Hardiness:	**Zones 7–9**
❄	Shape:	**Rounded**
🖌	Color:	**Red, pink, or white flower**
▦	Texture:	**Medium**
☼	Light:	**Light shade to part shade**
📏	Size:	**7–12 ft. high, 5–10 ft. wide**

Character:

Large evergreen shrub grown for winter flower in various colors, year-round foliage

Bawdy camellia dares to flower decadently in winter, but because of its timing, those flowers may be ruined by rain or frost, even where it's hardy. A favorite foundation plant in warm-climate gardens, especially in the South, camellia is tender north of Zone 7. Flowers range from white to pink to red.

STEWARTIA

Stewartia pseudocamellia

Hardiness:
Zones 5–9

Shape:
Pyramidal

Color:
White and yellow flower, white to brown bark, red fall leaf

Texture:
Medium

Light:
Full sun to part shade

Size:
12–40 ft. high, 8–25 ft. wide

Character:
Small deciduous tree or large shrub grown for white summer flower; red fall leaf, year-round white bark

Hardy stewartia grows to be a big shrub or little tree and wows year-round for its mottled white to brown peeling bark. Flowers appear in early summer, papery white with brilliant yellow centers. An easy-to-grow plant, stewartia needs average to moist soils and shade from hot afternoon sun.

SASANQUA CAMELLIA

Camellia sasanqua cultivars

Hardiness: **Zones 7–10**	Texture: **Medium, glossy**
Shape: **Rounded**	Light: **Light shade to part shade**
Color: **Red, pink, or white flower**	Size: **4–12 ft. high and wide**

Character:
Large evergreen shrub grown for fall flower in various colors, year-round foliage

Forever overshadowed by more popular *Camellia japonica*, sasanqua camellia flowers in vivid hues starting in fall, a more cooperative season for camellia bloom. Its leaves tend to be smaller, but deeper green, and more glossy than those of its cousin. Sasanquas take some drought once they're established.

CAMELLIA

APACHE PLUME

Fallugia paradoxa

Hardiness:
Zones 4–7

Texture:
Fine, soft

Shape:
**Rounded,
spreading**

Light:
Full sun

Color:
**White flower,
pink seedhead**

Size:
**2–6 ft. high,
5–8 ft. wide**

Character:
**Medium deciduous shrub grown
for pink spring and summer fruit,
white spring and summer flower,
as groundcover**

A tough, low-water native of the American West, all-star Apache plume is named for feathery pink seedheads that follow its gossamer white flowers, a showstopper in the garden for months on end. Apache plume grows like a champ in sun and well-drained soil. As a high-desert native, this cool plant takes heat and cold.

● ● ● ● ● ● ● ● ● ● ● ● ● ● ● ●

CRAPE MYRTLE

Lagerstroemia indica cultivars

🌡	Hardiness:	**Zones (6)7–9**
☁	Shape:	**Vase**
🔧	Color:	**White, pink, red, or lavender flower**
▦	Texture:	**Medium**
☼	Light:	**Full sun**
📏	Size:	**6–25 ft. high and wide**

Character:
Large deciduous shrub or small tree grown for summer flower in various colors

A one-time trendsetter, crape myrtle features as a foundation plant in three out of four gardens in the South, from formal to fetid. At its best, it's an elegant small tree with pretty bark and pink, purple, or white crepe-paper flowers in midsummer to fall. More often than not, it's ill-pruned, ill-fated, and ill-advised, and it's tender north of Zone 7.

JAPANESE TREE LILAC

Syringa reticulata

Hardiness:
Zones 3–7

Shape:
Oval

Color:
White flower

Texture:
Medium

Light:
Full sun to part shade

Size:
20–30 ft. high, 15–20 ft. wide

Character:
Small deciduous tree or large shrub grown for white summer flower

For cold-climate gardeners, Japanese tree lilac blooms in early summer with sprays of sweetly scented white flowers, the perfect foil to dashing, dark green leaves and cherry-brown bark. Larger and more regal than its shrubby lilac cousins, this plant comes without their pesky diseases too.

CRAPE MYRTLE

GIANT FLEECE FLOWER

Persicaria polymorpha

Hardiness:
Zones 4–9

Shape:
Rounded

Color:
White to pink flower

Texture:
Medium to bold in leaf, fine in flower

Light:
Full sun to part shade

Size:
3–6 ft. high and wide

Character:
Large herbaceous perennial grown for white to pink summer flower, size

Giant fleece flower is a big boy among garden perennials, but size-wise this plant fits perfectly on the scale of shrubs. In spring, it grows quick as a whip from the ground to 5 feet, and blooms white in summer, its flowers fading to shell pink in fall.

CHINESE INDIGO

Indigofera amblyantha

Hardiness:
Zones 6–9

Shape:
Rounded, open

Color:
Pink flower

Texture:
Fine

Light:
Full sun to part shade

Size:
4–10 ft. high and wide

Character:
Medium deciduous shrub grown for pink summer flower

Chinese indigo draws rave reviews from those in the know, with scores of dainty pink spires of bloom from spring to frost. This easy, low-water shrub may die to the ground in cold zones, but quickly regrows. It can be cut back in early spring for a sleeker silhouette throughout its range.

DAPHNE

Daphne species and cultivars

	Hardiness:	**Zones 4–8**
	Shape:	**Rounded to spreading**
	Color:	**White or pink flower**
	Texture:	**Fine to medium**
	Light:	**Part shade to full sun**
	Size:	**3–4 ft. high and wide**

Character:
Small to medium deciduous or semievergreen shrub grown for fragrant white or pink spring flower

Everybody wants a date with daphne, but daphne is notoriously fickle. Deliciously fragrant, daphne beguiles and baffles even advanced gardeners. It needs great drainage, some water (not too much), some sun (not too much), and protection from wind. Even then it may die a mysterious "daphne death," for reasons experts still only theorize.

CAROLINA ALLSPICE

Calycanthus floridus

Hardiness: **Zones 4–9**	Texture: **Medium to bold, glossy**
Shape: **Rounded, open**	Light: **Light shade to full sun**
Color: **Red or yellow-white flower (cultivar), yellow fall leaf**	Size: **6–10 ft. high, 6–12 ft. wide**

Character:
Medium deciduous shrub grown for fragrant red summer flower, yellow-white flower in cultivar

This southern belle's name says it all: the wine-red waterlily blooms of Carolina allspice smell of sweet, pungent tropical fruit, and its glossy leaves give off a spicy scent when crushed. Choose plants when blooming, as intensity of fragrance may vary. This adaptable native is cold-hardy to Zone 4. Cultivar 'Athens' blooms in an old-fashioned shade of linen.

SUMMERSWEET

Clethra alnifolia cultivars

Hardiness:
Zones 3–9

Shape:
Upright, oval

Color:
**White or pink
flower, yellow
fall leaf**

Texture:
Medium

Light:
**Part shade to
full sun**

Size:
**3–8 ft. high,
4–6 ft. wide**

Character:
**Medium deciduous shrub grown for
fragrant white or pink summer flower**

A midsummer night's dream in the scent of
spicy clove, summersweet's pink and white
cultivars of various sizes are sure to satisfy
any gardener. This native is a champ in average to wet soils, and flowers even in full shade.
'Rosea' (pictured) and 'Ruby Spice' bloom pink,
'Sixteen Candles' and 'Hummingbird' in white.

DAPHNE

SWEET OLIVE

Osmanthus fragrans

Hardiness:
Zones 8–10

Shape:
Rounded

Color:
White flower

Texture:
Medium

Light:
Part shade to full sun

Size:
8–15 ft. high and wide

Character:
Large deciduous shrub or small tree grown for fragrant fall to winter flower, year-round foliage, as hedge

An undervalued gem for warm zones, old-fashioned sweet olive's itsy-bitsy flowers may be the most powerfully fragrant for foundation or hedge plant available. More like holly than true olive, this all-star blooms fall into winter, takes heat, humidity, and shade, and grows readily in damp soil, but takes some drought once established.

DWARF RHODODENDRON

Rhododendron PJM Group

🌡	Hardiness:	**Zones 4–8**
🌿	Shape:	**Mounded**
🔌	Color:	**Pink to purple flower**
#	Texture:	**Medium**
☼	Light:	**Light shade to part shade**
📏	Size:	**3–6 ft. high and wide**

Character:

Medium evergreen shrub grown for pink to purple spring flower, year-round foliage, as hedge

PJM hybrids are a group of dwarf rhodies that are often planted, but rarely the life of the party. The plants bloom but once a year, in spring, before settling in as garden wallpaper. Like their parent, *Rhododendron carolinianum*, these hybrids like shade and acidic soil, but too often their popularity gets them planted and struggling in poor, sunny sites.

MOUNTAIN LAUREL

Kalmia latifolia cultivars

Hardiness:
Zones 3–9

Shape:
Mounded to irregular

Color:
Red, pink, or white flower, cinnamon bark

Texture:
Medium, glossy

Light:
Light shade to part shade

Size:
2–15 ft. high and wide

Character:

Medium evergreen shrub grown for spring flower in various colors, year-round foliage

Mountain laurel's defining characteristic is its flower: each one looks like a miniature overturned circus tent, with thousands frothing over from plants in early summer. This laurel is also valuable as an eastern native and for its cinnamon-colored bark. Many cultivars for size and color are available.

DWARF RHODO-DENDRON

SWAMP HONEYSUCKLE

Rhododendron viscosum and cultivars

Hardiness:
Zones 4–9

Shape:
Rounded

Color:
Pink, yellow, or white flower

Texture:
Medium

Light:
Full sun to part shade

Size:
4–8 ft. high and wide

Character:
Medium deciduous shrub grown for fragrant spring flower in various colors, red or orange fall foliage

A multiseason rhododendron, eastern native swamp honeysuckle is named for its tubular, gingerbread-scented flowers in late spring. Its deciduous foliage is an end-of-season blaze of orange and red in fall. This rhodie and its color cultivars ask only moist to average soil and shade in at least the heat of the day.

126

TEXAS RANGER

Leucophyllum frutescens and cultivars

Hardiness:
Zones (7)8–11

Texture:
Medium, soft

Shape:
Upright, mounded

Light:
Full sun to part shade

Color:
Pink, blue, purple, or white flower, silver leaf

Size:
8 ft. high and wide

Character:
Large evergreen shrub grown for pink, blue, purple, or white summer flower, year-round silver foliage, as hedge

Texas Ranger makes an all-star hedge for xeric gardens, bursting with bloom after summer rains. Its silver leaves make it a beacon in desert landscapes, and cultivars can be found for flower in pink, blue, purple, or white, and various sizes. Clumpy 'Compacta' trims up well as a hedge.

● ● ● ● ● ● ● ● ● ● ● ● ● ● ● ● ●

FORSYTHIA

Forsythia cultivars

🌡	Hardiness:	**Zones 5–8**
🌲	Shape:	**Upright, spreading**
🖌	Color:	**Gold flower, purple fall leaf**
⌗	Texture:	**Medium**
☼	Light:	**Full sun to full shade**
📏	Size:	**8–10 ft. high, 10–12 ft. wide**

Character:
Large deciduous shrub grown for yellow spring flower, as hedge

Wild child forsythia's brassy gold bursts forth on virtually every street corner in spring. It may fade into anonymity beyond that season, but forsythia grows big, wild, and woolly, much to the dismay of any admirer who attempts to tame it.

WINTER HAZEL

Corylopsis spicata and cultivars

Hardiness:
Zones 5–8

Shape:
Vase to spreading

Color:
Yellow flower, yellow leaf (cultivar), gold fall leaf

Texture:
Medium

Light:
Full sun to part shade

Size:
4–8 ft. high, 6–10 ft. wide

Character:
Medium to large deciduous shrub grown for fragrant yellow spring flower

Winter hazel strikes a refined note in spring, with delicate chains of pale, lemon-scented yellow flowers. This demure lady thrives in average garden conditions with afternoon shade. Cultivar 'Golden Spring' is a stunner with yellow foliage from spring to fall.

RED MAHONIA

Mahonia haematocarpa

Hardiness: **Zones 5–9**	Texture: **Medium, glossy**
Shape: **Upright, spreading**	Light: **Full sun to part shade**
Color: **Gold flower, red fruit**	Size: **8–12 ft. high, 10–12 ft. wide**

Character:
**Large evergreen shrub grown for gold
spring flower, year-round foliage, red
fall fruit, as hedge**

A drought-tolerant native of the Desert
Southwest, this big evergreen shines with gold
flowers in spring and red berries for birds in
fall. All it asks is good drainage. Red mahonia
grows at a restrained pace, but makes a great
hedge or screen in time.

129

FORSYTHIA

'SUNBURST' ST. JOHN'S WORT

Hypericum frondosum 'Sunburst'

Hardiness:
Zones 5–9

Shape:
Mounded, spreading

Color:
Gold flower, blue leaf

Texture:
Medium to fine

Light:
Full sun

Size:
3–4 ft. high and wide

Character:
Small deciduous shrub grown for gold summer flower, multiseason blue foliage, as groundcover

A galaxy of midsummer gold, the flowers of 'Sunburst' find a perfect foil in all-season blue foliage. This tidy cultivar of a Southeast native likes well-drained soil, fits well in small gardens, and can be cut to the ground in late winter in cold zones.

● ● ● ● ● ● ● ● ● ● ● ● ● ● ● ● ●

130

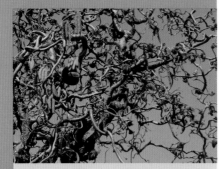

HARRY LAUDER'S WALKING STICK

Corylus avellana 'Contorta'

🌡	Hardiness:	**Zones 4–8**
🌳	Shape:	**Rounded, contorted**
⚡	Color:	**Brown flower, green leaf**
#	Texture:	**Fine in branch, medium in leaf**
☼	Light:	**Full sun to part shade**
📐	Size:	**8–10 ft. high and wide**

Character:
Large deciduous shrub grown for contorted shape

Harry Lauder's walking stick is great off-season eye candy, but like that cool kid with all the piercings, Harry may not age well. At summer's end, Harry's like a plant that just rolled out of bed, his leaves all shabby and rumpled. At worst, he sends up bushels of noncontorted suckers, each requiring removal.

CORKSCREW WILLOW

Salix 'Golden Curls' / *Salix* 'Scarlet Curls'

Hardiness:
Zones (4)5–8

Shape:
Upright, contorted

Color:
Yellow or red bark, green leaf

Texture:
Fine

Light:
Full sun to part shade

Size:
20–30 ft. high, 10–15 ft. wide

Character:
Small deciduous tree or large shrub grown for contorted shape, red or yellow bark year-round

Two hybrid willow cultivars make colorful, fast-growing shrubs for winter gardens and decorative cut branches: 'Golden Curls' (pictured), a coiled spectacle of red to gold, and 'Scarlet Curls', the same in crimson. Like all willows, both enjoy damp soil, but adapt to average garden conditions with gusto.

HARRY LAUDER'S WALKING STICK

CONTORTED FLOWERING QUINCE

Chaenomeles speciosa 'Contorta'

Hardiness:
Zones 5–9

Shape:
Rounded, contorted

Color:
Pink flower, green leaf

Texture:
Fine in branch, medium in leaf

Light:
Full sun to light shade

Size:
3–4 ft. high and wide

Character:
Medium deciduous shrub grown for pink spring flower, contorted shape

A fabulous twist on a classic shrub—literally—contorted quince's twisted form and pink to peach spring flowers make it a multiseason stunner in the garden. Like other quinces, 'Contorta' is adaptable, tough, and drought tolerant. Unlike its cousins, it's more petite, so it works better in smaller spaces.

CONTORTED HARDY ORANGE

Poncirus trifoliata 'Flying Dragon'

Hardiness:
Zones 6–10

Shape:
Rounded, contorted

Color:
Yellow fruit, white flower, green leaf

Texture:
Fine in branch, fine to medium in leaf

Light:
Full sun to part shade

Size:
3–6 ft. high and wide

Character:
Medium to large deciduous shrub grown for contorted shape, fragrant white spring flower, yellow summer fruit

Easy to grow most anywhere, this hardy citrus captivates with outsized, exotic thorns on top of contorted stems, winter standouts in glossy, dark green. Like its uncontorted parent, 'Flying Dragon' blooms sweetly in spring and bears sour fruit.

HOLLY

Ilex aquifolium

	Hardiness:	**Zones 7–9**
	Shape:	**Mounded, pyramidal**
	Color:	**Red fruit**
	Texture:	**Medium, glossy**
	Light:	**Full sun to part shade**
	Size:	**10–50 ft. high, 15–25 ft. wide; typically pruned to desired size**

Character:
Large evergreen shrub grown for year-round foliage, red fall fruit, as hedge

It may masquerade as a goody-two-shoes, its red berries shiny as patent leather, but make no mistake: English holly makes trouble. On the West Coast, it's an invasive species. In the hot, humid South, it gasps for breath, while in cold northern zones, it isn't hardy.

SNOWBERRY/ CORALBERRY

Symphoricarpos orbiculatus and cultivars
Symphoricarpos albus and cultivars

Hardiness: **Zones 2–10**	Texture: **Medium**
Shape: **Rounded, spreading**	Light: **Full sun to part shade**
Color: **Pink or white fruit**	Size: **2–6 ft. high, 4–8 ft. wide**

Character:
Small to medium deciduous shrub grown for pink or white fall fruit

This cheery crew of easy native shrubs grows across most of North America. Their fruit, borne late summer through winter, seems to drip from stems like shining beads of dew. Coralberry (*Symphoricarpos orbiculatus*) is showiest, with magenta fruit, while snowberry (*S. albus*, pictured) is famed for white.

HOLLY

LONGSTALK HOLLY

Ilex pedunculosa

Hardiness:
Zones 5–8

Shape:
Rounded

Color:
Red fruit

Texture:
Medium, glossy

Light:
Full sun to part shade

Size:
10–20 ft. high, 10–15 ft. wide

Character:
Medium to large evergreen shrub or small tree grown for year-round foliage, red fall fruit, as hedge

Longstalk holly may be the most underrated of broadleaf evergreens. In leaf, it's easily mistaken for weeping fig (*Ficus benjamina*), a popular houseplant. Grow male and female plants together, and in fall, females yield oversized red fruit that dangle from branches like cherries. Longstalk holly is easy to grow in average garden conditions.

AUCUBA

Aucuba japonica cultivars

Hardiness:
Zones (6)7–10

Shape:
Mounded, vase to irregular

Color:
Gold-variegated leaf, red fruit

Texture:
Bold, glossy

Light:
Light shade to full shade

Size:
6–10 ft. high and wide

Character:
Medium to large evergreen shrub grown for year-round variegated foliage, as hedge, red fall fruit

Aucuba livens up shady spots with fantastic foliage in a patina of golds and greens, and this tough shrub tackles heat, humidity, and drought to boot. An "almost tropical," it comes in cultivars big and small, and when grown with male plants, females produce red berries in fall.

HYDRANGEA

Hydrangea macrophylla cultivars

🌡	Hardiness:	**Zones 5–11**
☁	Shape:	**Rounded**
✂	Color:	**Pink or blue flower**
♯	Texture:	**Bold**
☀	Light:	**Light shade to full shade**
📐	Size:	**4–6 ft. high and wide**

Character:
Medium to large deciduous shrub grown for pink or blue summer flower

The moody ex-girlfriend of the plant world, hydrangea blooms mopheads of pink or blue, depending on soil pH. It wilts theatrically with too much sun and drought, and in cold climates its flowering buds often freeze. It's at its best in shady spots in warm, humid zones and coastal gardens.

'INVINCIBELLE SPIRIT' SMOOTH HYDRANGEA

Hydrangea arborescens 'Invincibelle Spirit'

Hardiness:	**Zones 3–9**
Shape:	**Rounded, spreading**
Color:	**Pink flower**
Texture:	**Medium, soft**
Light:	**Part shade**
Size:	**3–4 ft. high and wide**

Character:
Medium deciduous shrub grown for pink summer flower

Bubblegum pink 'Invincibelle Spirit' is a cultivar of white-flowered smooth hydrangea, a native of the eastern United States. Hardy to Zone 3, this hydrangea blooms in spite of cold, and its pink holds in spite of soil pH. Smooth hydrangea weathers short periods of drought better than its cousins do and does best with afternoon shade.

NANNYBERRY

Viburnum lentago

Hardiness:
Zones 2–8

Shape:
Upright

Color:
White flower, blue fruit, red fall leaf

Texture:
Medium to bold, glossy

Light:
Full sun to part shade

Size:
14–16 ft. high, 6–12 ft. wide

Character:
Large deciduous shrub grown for white spring flower, blue summer fruit, red fall foliage

Billowy white spring flowers and glossy leaves characterize nannyberry, named for goats' fondness of its blue fruit. (Birds love it too.) An eastern native, this low-water shrub thrives in climates nationwide. As a fall bonus, its deep green leaves turn to wine-colored shades of Shiraz.

139

HYDRANGEA

'BLUEBIRD' MOUNTAIN HYDRANGEA

Hydrangea serrata 'Bluebird'

Hardiness:
Zones 5–9

Shape:
Rounded, spreading

Color:
Blue or lavender flower

Texture:
Medium in leaf, fine in flower

Light:
Light shade to part shade

Size:
3–5 ft. high and wide

Character:
Small deciduous shrub grown for blue or lavender summer flower

The little hydrangea that could, compact 'Bluebird' shines in small spaces. Though it likes moist, fertile soil best, it takes to dry shade like a champ. A lacecap in bloom, with rings of big florets around filigreed centers, 'Bluebird' flowers blue in acidic soil, lavender-pink in alkaline.

JUNIPER

Juniperus ×pfitzeriana cultivars

	Hardiness:	**Zones 4–9**
	Shape:	**Spreading**
	Color:	**Green leaf**
	Texture:	**Fine, soft**
	Light:	**Full sun to light shade**
	Size:	**3–5 ft. high, 10–15 ft. wide**

Character:
Large evergreen shrub grown for year-round foliage, as hedge, fine texture, as groundcover

Shrubby juniper runs with a rough crowd of rugged plants, too often observed in parking lots and hell-strips, which doesn't endear it to many gardeners. Its large mature spread can come as a surprise too, as a small plant one year may quickly begin to eclipse its neighbors the next.

MUGO PINE

Pinus mugo cultivars

Hardiness:
Zones 2–7

Shape:
Upright, spreading

Color:
Green leaf

Texture:
Fine, soft

Light:
Full sun to light shade

Size:
5–6 ft. high and wide

Character:
Small to medium evergreen shrub grown for year-round foliage, fine texture, as groundcover

Like living candelabra, mugo pine brings unique form to gardens big and small, especially in cold climates. Varieties range in size from tiny ('Teeny', 1 foot or less) to bigger ('Mops', 4 feet) to biggest (var. *mugo*, 6 feet). All adapt to difficult sites and even take light shade.

JUNIPER

'GREY OWL' JUNIPER

Juniperus virginiana 'Grey Owl'

Hardiness:
Zones 2–9

Shape:
Spreading

Color:
Silver leaf

Texture:
Fine, soft

Light:
Full sun

Size:
**3–5 ft. high,
4–6 ft. wide**

Character:
**Small to medium evergreen shrub
grown for year-round silver foliage,
fine texture, as groundcover**

A spreading cultivar of native eastern red
cedar (*Juniperus virginiana*), glitzy 'Grey Owl'
might be better sold as silver. Its BB-like fruit
is edible bling for birds, and like its parent,
it thrives on tough sites in a huge range of
hardiness zones. At 6 feet, it's a more modest
spreader than more popular nonnatives.

'HOWELL'S DWARF TIGERTAIL' SPRUCE

Picea bicolor 'Howell's Dwarf Tigertail'

Hardiness:
Zones 4–7

Shape:
Spreading

Color:
Yellow to green leaf, purple fruit

Texture:
Fine in leaf, bold in cone, soft

Light:
Full sun

Size:
4–6 ft. high, 2–5 ft. wide

Character:
Small to medium evergreen shrub grown for year-round yellow to green leaf, purple spring fruit, fine texture, as groundcover

Yellow, green, blue, and violet: this pint-sized spruce is at the top of the conifer class. A spreading shrub, it's cloaked in needles of silvery blue-green, but spring growth emerges chartreuse, followed by cones in velvety purple. 'Tigertail' grows slowly, and makes an eye-catching specimen in gardens of all sizes.

143

LILAC

Syringa vulgaris cultivars

	Hardiness:	**Zones 3–7**
	Shape:	**Upright**
	Color:	**Pink, purple, or white flower**
	Texture:	**Medium**
	Light:	**Full sun**
	Size:	**6–12 ft. high and wide**

Character:
Large deciduous shrub grown for fragrant spring flower in various colors, as hedge

Lilac is the pretty girl from school who shows up at the reunion in sweats. It's a vision in spring, with clouds of fragrant flowers in cool colors. But lilac and humidity don't mix, so summer brings powdery mildew, even in cold climates where it grows well. Pruning is also a must, and spindly suckers are a pain.

KOREAN SPICE VIBURNUM

Viburnum carlesii

Hardiness:
Zones 4–7

Shape:
Upright to rounded, open

Texture:
Medium

Color:
Pink to white flower

Light:
Full sun to part shade

Size:
4–6 ft. high and wide

Character:
Medium deciduous shrub grown for fragrant pink to white summer flower, red fall foliage

If it's spring, you'll probably smell Korean spice viburnum before you see it. Beginning deep pink and aging to white, its blooms fill the air with a spicy clove scent and make great cut flowers. This shrub grows happily even in part shade, and its leaves stay clean and disease-free, turning to smoldering red in fall.

BUTTERFLY BUSH

Buddleia davidii cultivars

Hardiness:
Zones (5)6–9

Texture:
Medium

Shape:
Vase

Light:
Full sun

Color:
Pink, blue, purple, or white flower

Size:
6–8 ft. high, 3–5 ft. wide

Character:
Large deciduous shrub grown for fragrant summer flower in various colors

Butterfly bush loves heat in humid and dry climates, and this carefree beauty's sweetly-scented flowers make a show midsummer to fall, if deadheaded. Cut butterfly bush to the ground in late winter to keep up its elegant figure. It's a fabulous shrub everywhere but the Northwest, where it's an invasive species—gardeners there should avoid it.

LILAC

CALIFORNIA LILAC

Ceanothus thyrsiflorus and cultivars

Hardiness: **Zones 7–9**	Texture: **Fine to medium**
Shape: **Rounded, spreading**	Light: **Full sun**
Color: **Blue, lavender, or white flower**	Size: **4–12 ft. high, 6–20 ft. wide**

Character:
Small to large evergreen shrub grown for fragrant blue, lavender, or white summer flower, as hedge

The honey-scented spring flower of this western native is the stuff of legend, matched only by toughness and drought tolerance. Its many-sized cultivars mean there's one to fit any size garden. Pollinators adore its flowers, and birds relish its seeds.

● ● ● ● ● ● ● ● ● ● ● ● ● ● ● ● ●

PALM

Trachycarpus fortunei

🌡	Hardiness:	**Zones 7b–11**
🌿	Shape:	**Upright, symmetrical**
🖌	Color:	**Green leaf**
⊞	Texture:	**Bold, glossy**
☀	Light:	**Full sun to part shade**
📏	Size:	**20–35 ft. high, 8 ft. wide**

Character:
Small evergreen tree grown for bold texture, year-round foliage

At the track meet for tender tropicals we wish for most, windmill palm places a close second to banana. Hardiness aside, in reality, big palms look best in the neighbors' garden—up close, they're all trunk. Shrubby palms make a better fit for most gardens, but few of these prove cold-hardy either.

ARALIA

Aralia spinosa / Aralia elata cultivars

🌡 🌿 🖌 ⊞ ☀ 📏

Hardiness:
Zones 3–9

Shape:
Upright, symmetrical

Color:
White-variegated, gold-variegated, or green leaf, white flower, purple fruit

Texture:
Bold

Light:
Full sun to part shade

Size:
10–20 ft. high, 6–10 ft. wide

Character:
Large deciduous shrub or small tree grown for bold texture, symmetrical shape, multiseason foliage in various colors, white summer flower, purple fall fruit

Aralia dazzles with huge, leafy rosettes atop prickly canes, and galaxies of starry summer bloom. Berries follow soon after (birds too), especially in eastern native devil's walkingstick (*Aralia spinosa*). Variegated *A. elata* 'Silver Umbrellas' (pictured) and 'Aureovariegata' add colorful foliage. Aralia likes to spread out, so give it space.

PALM

STAGHORN SUMAC

Rhus typhina and cultivars

Hardiness:
Zones 3–8

Shape:
Upright, spreading; individual branchlets symmetrical

Color:
Green or gold leaf in cultivar, orange fall leaf

Texture:
Medium to bold, glossy

Light:
Full sun to part shade

Size:
6–25 ft. high, 6–30 ft. wide

Character:
Large deciduous shrub or small tree grown for bold texture, symmetrical shape, multiseason gold foliage in cultivar, orange fall foliage

Another plant that likes to colonize, native staghorn sumac is an A+ in the harshest conditions, and its glossy foliage and flocked red fruit feel right at home in faux tropical gardens. Smaller cultivar 'Tiger Eyes' (pictured) bewitches with gold to chartreuse foliage.

NEEDLE PALM

Rhapidophyllum hystrix

Hardiness:
Zones (6)7–10

Shape:
Symmetrical, rounded

Color:
Green leaf

Texture:
Bold, glossy

Light:
Light shade to full shade

Size:
3–6 ft. high and wide

Character:
Small evergreen shrub grown for bold texture, symmetrical shape, year-round foliage

Native to the Southeast, this hardiest of palms can be admired at eye level, growing slowly into a knot of glossy fronds. In snowy zones where it's maybe-hardy, adventurous gardeners should shop for larger plants, site in mild spaces, and protect them the first winter or two, until they've grown large enough to take the deep freeze.

PIERIS

Pieris japonica and cultivars

🌡	Hardiness:	**Zones 5–8**
🌲	Shape:	**Mounded, upright**
✂	Color:	**Red to green leaf, white flower**
▦	Texture:	**Medium, glossy**
☀	Light:	**Full sun to part shade**
📏	Size:	**4–12 ft. high, 3–8 ft. wide**

Character:
Medium evergreen shrub grown for red to green year-round foliage, white spring flower, as hedge

Ever the C student, pieris shines with care. Too often, it's a never-pruned foundation shrub, with weirdly irregular form and last year's pesky seed capsules. New growth can make for extreme red-green color contrast, and this evergreen may succumb to drying winter winds if sited badly.

ENKIANTHUS

Enkianthus campanulatus 'Showy Lantern'
Enkianthus campanulatus 'Red Bells'

Hardiness:
Zones 4–8

Shape:
Upright

Color:
Red flower, red fall leaf

Texture:
Medium in leaf, fine in flower

Light:
Full sun to part shade

Size:
6–10 ft. high, 4–6 ft. wide

Character:
Medium deciduous shrub grown for red spring flower, red fall foliage

Enkianthus blooms for ages in late spring with thousands of tiny bells on subtly architectural, upright stems. Foliage turns fiery crimson in fall. 'Showy Lantern' and 'Red Bells' are two colorful red-flowering cultivars. Enkianthus likes average to moist, acidic soil.

151

PIERIS

LEUCOTHOE

Leucothoe species and cultivars

Hardiness: **Zones 5–9**	Texture: **Medium, glossy**
Shape: **Spreading to mounded**	Light: **Light shade to full shade**
Color: **Green, white-variegated or red-variegated leaf in cultivars, white flower**	Size: **2–6 ft. high, 4–6 ft. wide**

Character:
Small to medium evergreen shrub grown for year-round foliage in various colors, white spring flower, as groundcover

Leucothoe (pron. loo-COH-thoh-ee) might be hard to say, but this native's rainbow of colorful varieties are among the easiest evergreens to love, and the most underrated. Tough and adaptable to a range of conditions, leucothoe spreads demurely and doubles as a groundcover. 'Rainbow' (pictured) features white-splashed foliage with red new growth; 'Scarletta' is a vision in crimson.

'ROBYN GORDON' GREVILLEA

Grevillea 'Robyn Gordon'

Hardiness:
Zones 9–10

Shape:
Mounded, spreading

Color:
Red flower, green leaf

Texture:
Fine, glossy

Light:
Full sun to light shade

Size:
5–6 ft. high, 8–10 ft. wide

Character:
Medium evergreen shrub grown for red spring to fall flower, as hedge, as groundcover

'Robyn Gordon' may be a popular gal in her native Australia, but this low-water shrub finds new fans in the United States all the time. Given poor, dry soil and great drainage, it fires off bristly, lipstick-red flowers for much of the year. Hummingbirds and bees flock to it from miles around.

● ● ● ● ● ● ● ● ● ● ● ● ● ● ● ● ●

PRIVET

Ligustrum vulgare / Ligustrum sinense

🌡	Hardiness:	**Zones 5–10**
☁	Shape:	**Vase to mounded**
🔌	Color:	**Green leaf, white flower**
﹟	Texture:	**Medium to fine**
☀	Light:	**Full sun to part shade**
📏	Size:	**6–20 ft. high, 6–10 ft. wide**

Character:
Large deciduous shrub or small tree grown as hedge, for fragrant white spring flower

Long the default for fast-growing deciduous hedge, privet eventually entered an elite group of troublemakers: those that are both overused and invasive species. Today, problem child privet upsets the balance of native ecosystems across the eastern United States, its seeds dispersed by birds.

ABELIA

Abelia ×grandiflora / Abelia mosanensis

Hardiness:
Zones 4–9

Shape:
Vase to mounded

Color:
Green leaf, pink or white flower

Texture:
Medium to fine, glossy

Light:
Full sun to part shade

Size:
3–6 ft. high and wide

Character:
Medium deciduous shrub grown for fragrant pink or white spring flower, as hedge, flower

A star among hedge plants, abelia exudes subtle grace. Drought tolerant and fast-growing, it shears great, blooms pink to white in spring and intermittently after. Fragrant flowers are a favorite of bees. Glossy abelia (*Abelia ×grandiflora*) thrives in warm climates, and fragrant abelia (*A. mosanensis*) as far north as Zone 4.

MOUNTAIN MAHOGANY

Cercocarpus species and cultivars

Hardiness:	**Texture:**
Zones 4–9	**Fine to medium, glossy in leaf, soft in flower**
Shape:	
Mounded to spreading	**Light:**
	Full sun to part shade
Color:	
Green leaf, brown fruit	**Size:**
	6–12 ft. high, 4–12 ft. wide

Character:
Medium evergreen shrub or small tree grown for year-round foliage, fine texture, brown summer fruit, as hedge

An evergreen of western deserts, mountain mahogany scoffs at extreme heat, cold, and drought. A fabulous accessorizer, in summer it cloaks itself in a robe of the finest feathery seeds. Cutleaf mountain mahogany (*Cercocarpus ledifolius*) bears small, glossy leaves, while the leaves of birchleaf (*C. betuloides* var. *blanchae*) resemble those of that tree.

PRIVET

KOHUHU

Pittosporum tenuifolium cultivars

Hardiness:
Zones 8–11

Shape:
Mounded to conical

Color:
Green or silver leaf, black bark

Texture:
Fine, glossy

Light:
Full sun to part shade

Size:
4–20 ft. high, 4–10 ft. wide

Character:
Small to large evergreen shrub or small tree grown for year-round green or silver foliage, as hedge

As hedges go, few bring as much shimmer to the garden as this pittosporum. Fast-growing, with tiny oval leaves on black stems, this pitt shears better than its big-leaved kin. 'Golf Ball' (pictured) stays small, while striking 'Silver Sheen' grows into a small tree if left unpruned.

PUSSY WILLOW

Salix discolor / Salix caprea

🌡	Hardiness:	**Zones 4–8**
🌲	Shape:	**Upright**
🔌	Color:	**Silver-white flower**
▦	Texture:	**Medium in leaf, fine and soft in flower**
☼	Light:	**Full sun to part shade**
📏	Size:	**6–25 ft. high, 4–15 ft. wide**

Character:
Large deciduous shrub or small tree grown for silver winter flower, fine texture

Beloved by flower arrangers, the fuzzy buds of pussy willow's powder-puff flowers are a treat in earliest spring. The show's over when this big shrub leafs out for the growing season—after that, it's just another face in the crowd.

FANTAIL WILLOW

Salix sacchalinensis 'Sekka'

🌡 🌲 🔌 ▦ ☼ 📏

Hardiness:
Zones 4–7

Shape:
Rounded

Color:
Silver-white flower, brown bark

Texture:
Medium, glossy in leaf, fine in flower and stem

Light:
Full sun to part shade

Size:
10–15 ft. high, 10–20 ft. wide

Character:
Large deciduous shrub grown for brown bark, silver winter flower, fine texture

Fantail willow makes things interesting all year. Fuzzy flowers appear in spring, but flattened, gnarled stems mean it's pretty for winter and offers cut branches year-round. Fantail's reedy leaves recall bamboo. Trim its oldest branches to the ground in late winter for the most and best stems for cutting.

PUSSY WILLOW

FOTHERGILLA

Fothergilla species and cultivars

Hardiness:
Zones 4–8

Shape:
Rounded to upright

Color:
White flower, blue leaf (cultivars), orange-red fall leaf

Texture:
Medium in leaf, soft in flower

Light:
Light shade to part shade

Size:
3–10 ft. high and wide

Character:
Large deciduous shrub grown for white flower, multiseason blue foliage in cultivars, orange-red fall foliage

A spectacular Southeast native, fothergilla bookends the growing season with fuzzy spring flowers and fabulous fall color. Dwarf fothergilla (*Fothergilla gardenii*) cultivars work for small spaces, while large fothergilla (*F. major*) fills the room. *Fothergilla gardenii* 'Blue Mist' and *F. ×intermedia* 'Blue Shadow' boast powder blue foliage to boot. All prefer some shade.

FOUNTAIN BUTTERFLY BUSH

Buddleia alternifolia

Hardiness: **Zones 5–10**	Texture: **Fine, soft**
Shape: **Vase to rounded, weeping**	Light: **Full sun**
Color: **Lavender flower, silver leaf (cultivar)**	Size: **8–20 ft. high and wide**

Character:
Large deciduous shrub grown for fragrant lavender spring flower, silver leaf in cultivar, fine texture

Fountain butterfly bush brightens any spring formal with long branches of lavender bunting. This easy, drought-tolerant shrub's weeping form is always pretty, and cultivar 'Argentea' is tricked out with silvery leaves all season. Prune old branches to the ground after it blooms for a new flush of growth.

● ● ● ● ● ● ● ● ● ● ● ● ● ● ● ● ● ●

159

PYRACANTHA

Pyracantha cultivars

🌡	Hardiness:	**Zones 5–9**
🌲	Shape:	**Mounded, spreading, irregular**
🖌	Color:	**Red or orange fruit**
▦	Texture:	**Fine, glossy**
☼	Light:	**Full sun**
📐	Size:	**6–12 ft. high and wide**

Character:
Medium evergreen or semi-evergreen shrub grown for red or orange fall fruit, white spring flower, fine texture, as hedge

For all the charms of its fiery-hued fall fruit, pyracantha is a bad boy who lives up to the thorny end of its name year-round. This shrub needs pruning and training to look its best, and its prickly disposition makes that chore not so pleasant. Hardiness can also be an issue at the top of its range.

WINTERBERRY

Ilex verticillata cultivars

Hardiness:
Zones 3–9

Texture:
Medium, glossy

Shape:
Vase to mounded

Light:
**Full sun to
part shade**

Color:
Red fruit

Size:
**3–10 ft. high
and wide**

Character:
**Medium deciduous shrub grown for
red winter fruit, as hedge**

Eastern native winterberry stops traffic every
fall, with red berries like tiny stoplights that
last through winter. This hardy, thornless holly
likes average to moist soils; it's even happy with
wet feet. Berries are food for overwintering
birds. Cultivars of various sizes are available.
Plant a one-to-nine male-to-female mix for fruit.

**PYRA-
CANTHA**

SEABERRY

Hippophae rhamnoides

Hardiness:
Zones 4–7

Texture:
Fine

Shape:
Open, spreading

Light:
Full sun

Color:
**Silver leaf,
orange fruit**

Size:
**10–25 ft. tall
and wide**

Character:
**Large deciduous shrub grown for
edible orange fall fruit, as hedge, fine
texture, multiseason silver foliage**

Seaberry grows vigorously in both cold climates
and harsh soils, and it produces cheerful,
edible orange fruit. A tall, silver-leaved shrub
with a busy root system that needs some
space, it thrives in salty seaside conditions too.
Male and female plants are a must for fruit.
Grow *en masse* for silver hedging.

POMEGRANATE

Punica granatum and cultivars

Hardiness:
Zones (7)8–11

Shape:
Mounded to vase

Color:
Orange to red flower, red or gold fruit

Texture:
Fine

Light:
Full sun

Size:
6–15 ft. high, 4–15 ft. wide

Character:
Medium to large evergreen or deciduous shrub grown for orange to red summer flower, edible red or gold fall fruit

Known for its edible fruit, low-water all-star pomegranate makes an awesome garden shrub. It flowers in vivacious red-orange throughout the growing season, and fall leaves are gold in climates where it goes deciduous. Fruit happens in long summer climates; dwarf variety *nana* fruits furthest north.

163

RHODODENDRON

Rhododendron large leaf cultivars

	Hardiness:	**Zones 5–7(8)**
	Shape:	**Rounded, irregular**
	Color:	**Red, pink, lavender, or white flower**
	Texture:	**Medium to bold**
	Light:	**Light shade to full shade**
	Size:	**4–10 ft. high, 4–12 ft. wide**

Character:
Large evergreen shrub grown for spring flower in various colors

Like its dwarf offspring in the PJM Group, conventional rhododendron makes for conventional planting in places where it's popular. Likes include long walks on the beach and blooming just once a year. Dislikes are hot climates, drought, and sun—even sun-tolerant varieties falter without enough moisture.

ROSEBAY

Rhododendron maximum

Hardiness:
Zones 3–7

Shape:
Rounded, spreading, open

Color:
Pink to white flower

Texture:
Medium to bold

Light:
Light shade to part shade

Size:
8–15 ft. high and wide

Character:
Large evergreen shrub, flower, hedge

Where popular rhodies are nonnative garden hybrids, rosebay is a multifaceted eastern native and supports all kinds of wildlife. It's the big shrub the kids will build an awesome fort inside, and it works great as an exotic screen. Rosebay likes moist to average soils and blooms pale pink early to midsummer, when other rhodies are toast.

'LITTLE GEM' MAGNOLIA

Magnolia grandiflora 'Little Gem'

Hardiness:
Zones (6)7–9

Shape:
Upright, oval

Color:
White flower, red fruit

Texture:
Medium to bold, glossy

Light:
Full sun to part shade

Size:
15–20 ft. high, 7–10 ft. wide

Character:
Large evergreen shrub or small tree grown for fragrant white summer flower, year-round foliage, as hedge, red fall fruit, size

A dwarf of towering southern magnolia, 'Little Gem' presents as large shrub in the garden. It is its native parent in miniature: glossy foliage year-round, fragrant flowers in summer, and striking red fall fruit. Its narrow silhouette makes it great for tight spaces.

RHODO-DENDRON

MEXICAN ORANGE

Choisya ternata and cultivars

Hardiness:
Zones 8–10

Shape:
Mounded

Color:
White flower, gold leaf (cultivar)

Texture:
Medium, glossy

Light:
Full sun to light shade

Size:
6–8 ft. high and wide

Character:
Medium evergreen shrub grown for fragrant white spring flower, year-round foliage, as hedge, yellow foliage in cultivar

Mexican orange makes a party of any foundation planting. It's fast-growing and drought tolerant, has glossy foliage, and produces fragrant white flowers in spring. Cultivar 'Sundance' one-ups its parent with new growth in vivid chartreuse, while hybrid 'Aztec Pearl' has pink buds and a more demure silhouette.

• • • • • • • • • • • • • • • • • • • •

ROSE—HYBRID TEA

Rosa cultivars

Hardiness: **Zones 5–10**

Shape: **Upright, irregular**

Color: **Red, pink, yellow, lavender, or white flower**

Texture: **Medium**

Light: **Full sun**

Size: **3–5 ft. high and wide**

Character:
Small to medium deciduous shrub grown for fragrant multiseason flower in various colors, fragrance

Hybrid tea rose is the queen of the fussy plant prom. Unless it's preened and pruned, prickly rose becomes HQ for a who's who of pests and diseases. Too often, poisonous chemicals are the only remedy for these, as well as fertilizer, if the plant is to look its best.

'MINIATURE SNOWFLAKE' MOCK ORANGE

Philadelphus ×virginalis 'Miniature Snowflake'

Hardiness: **Zones 4–8**

Shape: **Upright, vase**

Color: **White flower**

Texture: **Medium**

Light: **Full sun to part shade**

Size: **3–4 ft. high and wide**

Character:
Small deciduous shrub grown for fragrant white spring flower

A low-care plant that grows almost anywhere, this dwarf mock orange explodes in a sweet-smelling surge of white flowers in late spring. Its foliage is a pristine dark green that stays fresh all through the growing season. Prune older shoots to the ground after it blooms for a more compact plant.

ROSE— HYBRID TEA

ROSE—LOW-CARE SHRUBS

Rosa cultivars

Hardiness:
Zones 5–10

Shape:
Upright, irregular

Color:
Red, pink, yellow, or white flower

Texture:
Medium

Light:
Full sun to light shade

Size:
2–4 ft. high and wide

Character:
Small to medium deciduous shrub grown for multiseason flower in various colors

Rose lovers rejoice! The recent popularity of low-care shrub roses means a flood of great varieties is available. All virtually thrive on neglect, and many bloom all season. Two of the best are *Rosa* The Knock Out series and *Rosa* Oso Easy series. *Rosa* 'The Fairy', also known as sweetheart rose, and its kin work well in smaller gardens.

ROCK ROSE

Cistus species, hybrids, and cultivars

Hardiness: **Zones 8–10**	Texture: **Medium**
Shape: **Upright or prostrate, spreading**	Light: **Full sun**
	Size: **2–6 ft. high, 4–7 ft. wide**
Color: **Pink, purple, or white flower**	

Character:
Medium evergreen shrub grown for spring flower in various colors, as groundcover

Rock rose is as carefree as its namesake is not. It's a low-water shrub, blooms spring to early summer, and comes in all sizes: low growers for groundcover and smaller gardens, and shrubby varieties for height. Of the big plants, purple *Cistus ×purpureus* shines, while pink *C.* 'Sunset' leads the minis.

● ● ● ● ● ● ● ● ● ● ● ● ● ● ● ● ●

SCOTCH BROOM

Cytisus scoparius cultivars

	Hardiness:	**Zones 5–8**
	Shape:	**Vase**
	Color:	**Yellow, white, orange, or pink flower**
	Texture:	**Fine, soft**
	Light:	**Full sun**
	Size:	**4–8 ft. high and wide**

Character:

Medium deciduous shrub grown for fragrant yellow spring flower, fine texture

The shrub voted "Most Likely to Incite Biological Warfare" by western gardeners, Scotch broom grows like a weed most anywhere, but makes the most trouble in the West, where it threatens native ecosystems all along the Pacific coast. Its fragrant spring flowers sparkle innocently in gold, and cultivars bloom in shades from creamy white to orange to deep rose.

KERRIA

Kerria japonica and cultivars

Hardiness:
Zones 4–9
Shape:
Vase, spreading
Color:
Yellow flower
Texture:
Fine
Light:
Part shade
Size:
4–8 ft. high, 5–9 ft. wide

Character:
Medium deciduous shrub grown for yellow spring flower

A wonderfully foolproof star for shade, vigorous kerria delights across a huge range of climates with sprays of gold spring daisies. Delicate but durable, kerria makes the grade even in full shade. 'Golden Guinea' blooms biggest and brightest. 'Picta' is less hearty, but its variegated leaves light up shady spaces all season long.

DAPPLED WILLOW

Salix integra 'Hakuro-nishiki'

Hardiness:	Texture:
Zones 4–9	**Medium, soft**

Shape:	Light:
Vase to rounded	**Full sun to part shade**

Color:	
Pink to white-variegated leaf	

	Size:
	4–6 ft. high, 5–7 ft. wide

Character:
Medium deciduous shrub grown for multiseason variegated foliage, fine texture, as hedge

Dappled willow throws a coming out party every spring, with fountains of new foliage in soft pink that age and mingle with white-splashed green, and the show goes on 'til fall. This versatile willow will grow as a large shrub, or, if cut to the ground in late winter, regrow in a spectacular color show each year.

**SCOTCH
BROOM**

BUSH CLOVER

Lespedeza thunbergii cultivars

Hardiness:
Zones 5–9

Light:
**Full sun to
part shade**

Shape:
Vase

Size:
**4–5 ft. high,
5–10 ft. wide**

Color:
**Pink or white
flower**

Texture:
**Medium in
leaf, fine and
soft in flower**

Character:
**Medium deciduous shrub grown
for pink or white summer flower;
fine texture**

Bush clover ranks among the top "parking lot
plants" across climates, yet remains an underused gem in American gardens. One of the
brightest stars in the late summer pep squad,
it has cultivars in purple, pink, and white.
Vigorous and drought tolerant, bush clover is
most tidy when cut to the ground each winter
and allowed to regrow.

SPIREA

Spiraea japonica cultivars

	Hardiness:	**Zones 4–8**
	Shape:	**Mounded, spreading**
	Color:	**Pink or white flower, gold leaf in cultivars**
	Texture:	**Medium in leaf, fine in flower, soft**
	Light:	**Full sun to part shade**
	Size:	**2–3 ft. high, 3–5 ft. wide**

Character:
Small to medium deciduous shrub grown for pink or white summer flower, fine texture, multiseason gold foliage in cultivars, as groundcover

Common to the point of overplay, Japanese spirea is the DJ you hire when you can't afford the band. Its pink clusters in early summer are a once-a-year trick, although many varieties also make new foliage in neon yellow—an eye-popping contrast that's more trippy than attractive.

HARDHACK SPIREA

Spiraea douglasii / Spiraea tomentosa

Hardiness:
Zones 3–8

Shape:
Upright, spreading

Color:
Pink flower

Texture:
Medium in leaf, fine in flower; soft

Light:
Full sun to part shade

Size:
2–6 ft. high, 3–6 ft. wide

Character:
Medium deciduous shrub grown for pink summer flower; fine texture

Please direct your attention to two native spireas: one from the West (*S. douglasii*) and one the East (*S. tomentosa*). Both are called hardhack, and both bear fuzzy pink paintbrushes of flower in early summer, favorites of beneficial insects. Both like average to wet soils and spread modestly, but not uncontrollably.

SPIREA

DEUTZIA

Deutzia gracilis and cultivars

Hardiness:
Zones 5–8

Shape:
Rounded

Color:
White flower, gold leaf in cultivar

Texture:
Medium in leaf, fine in flower

Light:
Full sun to part shade

Size:
2–5 ft. high and wide

Character:
Small deciduous shrub grown for fragrant white spring flower, multiseason gold foliage in cultivar, fine texture, as groundcover

Deutzia bursts into bloom spring to early summer with a zillion sweet-smelling white bells, and cultivar 'Chardonnay Pearls' (pictured) ups the ante with coordinated citron-colored foliage that keeps things interesting all season. Dapper deutzia adapts well most anywhere.

CEANOTHUS

Ceanothus ×pallidus 'Marie Simon'
Ceanothus ×pallidus 'Marie Bleu'

Hardiness:
Zones 5–10

Shape:
Rounded to spreading

Color:
Pink or blue flower

Texture:
Medium in leaf, fine in flower, soft

Light:
Full sun

Size:
3–5 ft. high and wide

Character:
Small to medium deciduous shrub grown for pink or blue summer flower, fine texture

Most ceanothus grow only on the West Coast, but don't tell these cultivars—they flourish in poor soil in a range of climates, asking only good drainage. 'Marie Simon' (pictured) flowers in summer in pink, 'Marie Bleu' in blue. In cold climates, plants can be cut back to the ground in late winter.

● ● ● ● ● ● ● ● ● ● ● ● ● ● ●

175

YEW

Taxus species and cultivars

🌡	Hardiness:	**Zones 4–7**
🌲	Shape:	**Mounded, upright, spreading or prostrate**
🍃	Color:	**Green leaf**
▦	Texture:	**Fine, glossy**
☼	Light:	**Full sun to full shade**
📏	Size:	**2–25 ft. high and wide; typically pruned to desired size**

Character:
Medium to large evergreen shrub or small tree grown for year-round foliage, as hedge

Ever popular in the Northeast for hedge, screen, or spreading evergreen, yew fights a losing battle with extreme heat and dislikes drought both in winter and summer. In regions where its needs are met, it proves amazingly adaptable, but rarely inspiring.

GOLD-LEAVED YEW

Taxus baccata 'Repandens Aurea'
Taxus cuspidata 'Dwarf Bright Gold'

Hardiness: **Zones 4–7**	Texture: **Fine, glossy**
Shape: **Mounded, upright or spreading**	Light: **Full sun to part shade**
Color: **Gold to green leaf**	Size: **2–6 ft. high, 2–10 ft. wide**

Character:
Medium evergreen shrub grown for year-round gold to green foliage, as hedge

For something yew-like yet completely different, two cultivars strike gold: 'Repandens Aurea' the low-growing, spreading type, and 'Dwarf Bright Gold' (pictured), a bushier variety. From spring into summer, both show off in new outfits of a sunny yellow (more chartreuse in shade), before aging gracefully to green.

YEW

PLUM YEW

Cephalotaxus harringtonia and cultivars

Hardiness:
Zones 6–9

Texture:
Fine, glossy

Shape:
Mounded, columnar or prostrate

Light:
Light shade to full shade

Color:
Green leaf

Size:
5–10 ft. high and wide

Character:
Medium to large evergreen shrub grown for year-round foliage, as hedge, as groundcover, prostrate or columnar shape in cultivars

A graceful yew cousin, plum yew is at home in hot, humid climates and cold zones, and comes in two great forms: 'Prostrata' (pictured), a spreader, doubles as a groundcover, and 'Fastigiata', an upright, columnar form, is good as screening in groups or alone as a striking specimen.

JAPANESE YEW

Podocarpus species and cultivars

Hardiness:	Light:	Character:
Zones 8–11	**Full sun to full shade**	**Large evergreen shrub grown for year-round green leaf or blue leaf in cultivar, as hedge**
Shape:		
Upright	Size:	
Color:	**10–40 ft. high, 10–25 ft. wide; typically pruned to lesser size**	
Green or blue leaf (cultivar)		
Texture:		
Fine, glossy		

If foliage trends larger in the tropics, this holds true for this yew, a hot-zone conifer whose long, needlelike leaves are yew writ large and distinguish it from *Taxus cuspidata*, which also goes by "Japanese yew." This evergreen wows as warm-climate screen or hedge and comes in varieties of various sizes. Cultivar 'Icee Blue' boasts sensationally steely blue foliage.

Boston ivy (*Parthenocissus tricuspidata*) beats the pants off of English ivy (*Hedera helix*) for color in the fall garden.

Vines

Not to be forgotten on the garden playground, vines are the kids in constant competition with trees and shrubs for the title of "Most Popular," forever climbing and scrambling through the crowd. At their best, they can be the garden's crown jewels. All too often, their zeal to reach the top gets the best of them, and they run rampant over their peers. Which vines play nice, and which are vines of vice? Here are a group of troublemakers best avoided, along with all-star problem-solvers more likely to succeed.

EVERYDAY PROBLEM

ASIAN BITTERSWEET

Celastrus orbiculatus

Hardiness:	**Zones 4–8**
Shape:	**Tendril/ twining vine**
Color:	**Red-orange fruit**
Texture:	**Medium in leaf, fine in fruit**
Light:	**Full sun to full shade**
Size:	**30 ft. or more high**

Character:
Large deciduous woody vine grown for red-orange fall fruit

A favorite with flower arrangers for its red-orange fall fruit, Asian bittersweet wants to be the cold-climate kudzu *(Pueraria lobata)* when it grows up. It gobbles up fields and forests all over the East, leaving room for little else to grow. It's often sold mistakenly as native American bittersweet (*Celastrus scandens*).

EXTRAORDINARY ALTERNATIVES

'MORNING CALM' CHINESE TRUMPET CREEPER

Campsis grandiflora 'Morning Calm'

Hardiness:
Zones 6–9

Shape:
Clinging vine

Color:
Red-orange flower

Texture:
Medium

Light:
Full sun to part shade

Size:
20–25 ft. high

Character:
Large deciduous woody vine grown for red-orange summer flower

Wild child trumpet creeper will be familiar to many gardeners, but 'Morning Calm' Chinese creeper tames more easily and comes with cheery flowers in a deeper shade of apricot-orange. It blooms in early summer and reblooms in short bursts until fall.

CROSS VINE

Bignonia capreolata 'Tangerine Beauty'

Hardiness:	Texture:
Zones 5–9	**Medium, glossy**
Shape:	Light:
Clinging vine	**Full sun to part shade**
Color:	
Red-orange flower	Size:
	20–30 ft. high

Character:
Large deciduous woody vine grown for red-orange spring flower

A native of the Southeast and lower Midwest, cross vine shines with leathery, dark green leaves and luscious late spring flowers, at their most vivid in red-orange in 'Tangerine Beauty'. Cross vine will climb to the treetops, so plant on lower structures for best viewing, and prune post-bloom to keep it in line.

183

ASIAN BITTER-SWEET

GLORIOSA LILY

Gloriosa superba

Hardiness:
Zones 8–10

Shape:
Tendril/ twining vine

Color:
Red and yellow flower

Texture:
Medium in leaf, fine in flower

Light:
Full sun to part shade

Size:
5–6 ft. high, 1–3 ft. wide

Character:
Small herbaceous vine grown for red and yellow multiseason flower

Gloriosa may be a lily, but it climbs with the best of vines. This twiner blooms red and yellow throughout warm months in mild climates, its weird, wonderful flowers like two-toned trumpets turned inside out. In Zone 8, the top of its range, it dies to the ground in winter, returning in spring.

CLEMATIS—
LARGE-FLOWERED

Clematis, large-flowered species and cultivars

	Hardiness:	**Zones 4–8**
	Shape:	**Tendril/ twining vine**
	Color:	**Red, pink, blue, purple, or white flower**
	Texture:	**Medium to bold**
	Light:	**Full sun to part shade**
	Size:	**6–10 ft. high and wide**

Character:
Medium herbaceous vine grown for multiseason flower in various colors

An old-fashioned beauty, large-flowered clematis cultivars bloom from late spring to late summer. Clematis does best with its face to the sun and its roots in cool, not-too-dry shade. If it's stressed, it's more prone to a common, unpretty disease called clematis wilt.

VIRGIN'S BOWER

Clematis virginiana

Hardiness:	**Zones 3–8**
Shape:	**Tendril/ twining vine**
Color:	**White flower**
Texture:	**Medium to fine, soft**
Light:	**Full sun to part shade**
Size:	**12–20 ft. high, 3–6 ft. wide**

Character:
Large herbaceous vine grown for fragrant white fall flower

A native plant east of the Rockies, virgin's bower blooms like crazy just when most gardens need some freshening up. Its cascades of small, sweetly fragrant white flowers turn to pompons of seeds, extending the show to frost. This and other small-flowered varieties are less prone to clematis wilt.

CLEMATIS— LARGE- FLOWERED

'ROOGUCHI' CLEMATIS

Clematis integrifolia 'Rooguchi'

Hardiness:
Zones 4–9

Shape:
Tendril/ twining vine

Color:
Blue to purple flower

Texture:
Medium

Light:
Full sun to part shade

Size:
6 ft. high and wide

Character:
Medium herbaceous vine grown for blue to purple multiseason flower

Dainty 'Rooguchi' blooms in an ocean of violet-blue from spring all the way to fall, no wilt in sight. Topping out at 6 feet, it works well in any size garden. 'Rooguchi' needs support, so grow it through shrubs or small structures, and give it afternoon shade in hot climates. It dies to the ground in winter.

ZIMBABWE CREEPER

Podranea ricasoliana

Hardiness:	Light:
Zones 8–11	**Full sun to part shade**
Shape:	
Clinging vine	Size:
Color:	**16–20 ft. high and wide**
Pink flower	
Texture:	
Medium to bold	

Character:
Large evergreen or deciduous woody vine grown for fragrant pink multiseason flower

A big vine with a taste for adventure, fast-growing Zimbabwe creeper rewards mild-climate gardeners with rafts of vanilla-scented trumpets up to 10 feet long. It blooms all season in frost-free zones, late summer in cooler Zone 8. Shear it back to central stems once a year to keep it in check, or just let it go.

CLIMBING ROSE

Rosa cultivars

	Hardiness:	**Zones 5–9**
	Shape:	**Rambling vine**
	Color:	**Red, pink, yellow, lavender, or white flower**
	Texture:	**Medium**
	Light:	**Full sun**
	Size:	**8–12 ft. high, 3–6 ft. wide**

Character:

Medium deciduous woody vine grown for fragrant multiseason flower in various colors

Climbing roses can be chemically dependent divas as much as their earthbound cousins, only taller. Ignore them and they become a hub of pests, too often requiring treatment with noxious chemicals to keep them up. Like other roses, they also need pruning, deadheading, and fertilization.

PRAIRIE ROSE

Rosa setigera

Hardiness:
Zones 5–9

Shape:
Rambling vine

Color:
Pink flower, red-purple fall leaf, red fruit

Texture:
Medium

Light:
Full sun

Size:
6–12 ft. high, 8–10 ft. wide

Character:

Medium deciduous woody vine grown for fragrant pink spring flower, red fall fruit

A single-flowered rose that blooms in a late-spring spectrum of pink, prairie rose also features red-purple fall foliage and red fruit. This Midwest native resists pests and diseases better than nonnative garden varieties. A rambler, it likes sun and average soil, and it's easy to train up an arbor or trellis.

'BALLERINA' ROSE

Rosa 'Ballerina'

Hardiness:	Texture:
Zones 5–9	**Medium**
Shape:	Light:
Rambling vine	**Full sun**
Color:	Size:
Pink flower	**4–6 ft. high and wide**

Character:
Small to medium deciduous woody vine grown for fragrant pink multiseason flower

Lusty 'Ballerina' blooms with blousy bouquets of pale pink—especially in spring, but throughout the season—shows great resistance to pests and diseases, and thrives in sun or light shade. An old-fashioned hybrid musk rose, its flowers are lightly fragrant, and it trains easily up, up and away.

CLIMBING ROSE

'PEGGY MARTIN' ROSE

Rosa 'Peggy Martin'

Hardiness:
Zones 5–9

Shape:
Rambling vine

Color:
Pink flower

Texture:
Medium

Light:
Full sun

Size:
10–15 ft. high and wide

Character:
Medium deciduous woody vine grown for pink multiseason flower

One of two plants that survived a 20-foot flood of saltwater in the Louisiana garden of its namesake after Hurricane Katrina, 'Peggy Martin' is a tough customer with an amazing story. Today, this brilliant pink climber's offspring will surely be tough enough to thrive in your garden. All 'Peggy' needs is sun, and she's happy.

190

ENGLISH IVY

Hedera helix

🌡	Hardiness:	**Zones 4–9**
🍃	Shape:	**Clinging vine**
🔌	Color:	**Green or variegated leaf (cultivars)**
#	Texture:	**Medium, glossy**
☼	Light:	**Full sun to full shade**
📏	Size:	**20–80 ft. high, 10–50 ft. wide**

Character:
Large evergreen vine grown for clinging shape, year-round foliage, variegated in cultivars, as groundcover

In the school of plants, English ivy might just graduate to the Ivy League if it weren't so bent on world domination. Left unchecked, this ivy quickly overruns its borders and merits "invasive species" status in forests across North America, where it's known to tackle mature trees.

BOSTON IVY

Parthenocissus tricuspidata

Hardiness:
Zones 4–8

Shape:
Clinging vine

Color:
Green leaf, red fall leaf

Texture:
Medium to bold, glossy

Light:
Full sun to full shade

Size:
30–50 ft. high, 5–10 ft. wide

Character:
Large deciduous vine grown for clinging shape, red fall foliage

Most of the year, Boston ivy is best known as a tidy, glossy-leaved climber, useful as uniform vertical carpeting for walls—until fall, when its leaves turn a spectacular red. Boston ivy grows well in sun or shade, but colors up best in full sun. Prune to keep it in check.

**ENGLISH
IVY**

VIRGINIA CREEPER

Parthenocissus quinquefolia

Hardiness:
Zones 4–9

Shape:
Clinging vine

Color:
**Variegated leaf,
red fall leaf**

Texture:
Medium to fine

Light:
**Full sun to
part shade**

Size:
**20–30 ft. high,
5–10 ft. wide**

Character:
**Large deciduous woody vine grown
for clinging shape, multiseason
variegated foliage in cultivars, red
fall foliage**

Though its name says Virginia, this creeper is
native to the whole of eastern North America.
It is a cinch to grow in average conditions, and
its variegated cultivars make mild-mannered
garden additions. Both 'Variegata' and 'Star
Showers' (pictured) sport white-dappled foliage and gorgeous red-orange fall color.

'MOONLIGHT' CLIMBING HYDRANGEA

Schizophragma hydrangeoides 'Moonlight'

Hardiness:
Zones 5–9

Shape:
Clinging vine

Color:
Silver-blue to green leaf, white flower

Texture:
Medium to fine

Light:
Light shade to full shade

Size:
20–30 ft. high, 6–10 ft. wide

Character:
Large deciduous woody vine grown for silver-blue to green leaf, white summer flower, clinging shape

For fabulous foliage and flower in a trouble-free vine, 'Moonlight' hydrangea is an all-star at its best. A refined beauty for shade, 'Moonlight' boasts luminous silvery blue leaves throughout the growing season, and hydrangea-like lacecap bouquets of white flowers with age.

JAPANESE HONEYSUCKLE

Lonicera japonica

	Hardiness:	**Zones 5–9**
	Shape:	**Tendril/ twining vine**
	Color:	**White to yellow flower**
	Texture:	**Medium**
	Light:	**Full sun to part shade**
	Size:	**20–30 ft. high and wide**

Character:
Large deciduous woody vine grown for fragrant white to yellow summer flower, twining shape

Sweetly scented though it may be in summer, Japanese honeysuckle makes trouble across the entire eastern half of the United States and parts of the West. This woody vine runs rampant as an invasive species, upending all manner of ecosystems.

'KINTZLEY'S GHOST' GRAPE HONEYSUCKLE

Lonicera reticulata 'Kintzley's Ghost'

Hardiness:	Texture:
Zones 4–8	**Medium, soft**
Shape:	Light:
Tendril/ twining vine	**Full sun to light shade**
Color:	Size:
Yellow and silver-blue flower	**10–15 ft. high and wide**

Character:
Large deciduous woody vine grown for yellow and silver-blue multiseason flower, twining shape

A knockout cultivar of a Midwest native, 'Kintzley's Ghost' blooms pale yellow in spring. Flowers are backed by silver-blue bracts like eucalyptus leaves, and these keep the show going over the whole growing season. Low-water 'Kintzley's Ghost' grows easily in sun and average conditions.

'MAJOR WHEELER' CORAL HONEYSUCKLE

Lonicera sempervirens 'Major Wheeler'

Hardiness:
Zones 4–9

Shape:
Tendril/ twining vine

Color:
Red flower

Texture:
Medium

Light:
Full sun to light shade

Size:
15–20 ft. high and wide

Character:
Large deciduous woody vine grown for red multiseason flower, twining shape

A cultivar of East and Midwest native coral honeysuckle, 'Major Wheeler' puts on the Ritz late spring in ravishing red and resists mildew better than its parent. Hummingbirds adore its flowers. Trim 'Wheeler' a bit after each bloom, and it keeps blooming, at a modest pace, all the way to fall.

JAPANESE HONEY-SUCKLE

CALIFORNIA HONEYSUCKLE

Lonicera hispidula

Hardiness: **Zones 5–9**	Texture: **Medium**
Shape: **Tendril / twining vine**	Light: **Full sun to part shade**
Color: **Pink flower, red fruit**	Size: **15–20 ft. high and wide**

Character:
Large deciduous woody vine grown for fragrant pink summer flower, twining shape, red fall fruit

True to its name, all-star California honeysuckle hails from the West Coast. This pretty low-water vine not only blooms pink in summertime, it also follows up with red berries—the former a boon to hummingbirds, the latter to other birds.

● ● ● ● ● ● ● ● ● ● ● ● ● ● ● ● ● ● ●

WISTERIA

Wisteria sinensis

	Hardiness:	**Zones 5–9**
	Shape:	**Tendril/ twining vine**
	Color:	**Lavender flower**
	Texture:	**Medium to fine**
	Light:	**Full sun**
	Size:	**10–30 ft. high and wide**

Character:
Large deciduous woody vine grown for fragrant lavender spring flower, twining shape

Rowdy kid wisteria has a reputation for trouble going back generations. Today, this classic-but-chaotic climber has escaped into forests, where it chokes trees and blocks light from plants on the forest floor. Its spring perfume and purple chains of bloom still entice gardeners.

GROUNDNUT

Apios americana

Hardiness:
Zones 5–9

Shape:
Tendril / twining vine

Color:
Pink flower

Texture:
Medium to fine

Light:
Full sun to part shade

Size:
15–20 ft. high and wide

Character:
Large deciduous woody vine grown for fragrant pink fall flower, twining shape

An adaptable native of the East and Midwest, groundnut belies its ho-hum name with intricate, fragrant, wisteria-like flowers of red-purple in late summer, each like a little chain of seashells. True to its name, this vigorous vine's roots are edible, each like a little potato.

WISTERIA

AMERICAN WISTERIA

Wisteria frutescens

Hardiness:	Texture:	Character:
Zones 5–9	**Medium to fine**	**Large deciduous woody vine grown for fragrant lavender spring flower, twining shape**
Shape:	Light:	
Tendril/ twining vine	**Full sun**	
Color:	Size:	
Lavender flower	**20–30 ft. high, 4–8 ft. wide**	

American wisteria grows at a more modest clip than Asian *Wisteria sinensis*; more than that, it's a native plant of the East and Midwest. This wisteria blooms in fragrant, jewel-toned purple in spring, after its leaves have emerged, and grows easily in sun and average soil.

CORAL PEA

Hardenbergia violacea

Hardiness:
Zones 9–11

Texture:
Medium to fine

Shape:
**Tendril /
twining vine**

Light:
**Full sun to
part shade**

Color:
Lavender flower

Size:
**10–15 ft. high
and wide**

Character:
**Large evergreen woody vine grown
for lavender spring flower, twining
shape, year-round foliage**

In mild climates, from late winter to early
spring, elegant fountains of purple cascade
over coral pea's evergreen willow-like leaves.
This low-water Australian vine grows at a
manageable clip, and it's happiest with shade
in the hottest part of the day.

● ● ● ● ● ● ● ● ● ● ● ● ● ● ● ● ● ●

Colorful fleece flower (*Persicaria microcephala*
'Red Dragon') has all the pretty foliage of a canna,
but comes back in cold climates.

Perennials

Perennials are the most complicated kids in the garden schoolyard. They come in sizes big and small, and while some may stick around year-round, others may die back in winter. Whatever their temperament, perennials need not be complicated to grow—indeed, although some can be fussy, as a group, they may be the most adaptable bunch in the plant world. Let's look at which perennials aren't worth your while, and a star-studded lineup of alternatives for each.

AGAVE

Agave species

Hardiness:	**Zones 8–11**	
Shape:	**Spiky rosette**	
Color:	**Blue leaf**	
Texture:	**Bold, soft**	
Light:	**Full sun**	
Size:	**3–6 ft. high, 6–10 ft. wide**	

Character:
Large evergreen succulent grown for bold texture, spiky rosette shape, year-round blue foliage

Agave (pron. ah-gah-VEH) makes a dramatic rosette of striking, fleshy, powder-blue leaves. As a succulent, it stores too much liquid in those leaves to abide the deep freeze of cold, damp climates. A desert inhabitant, it thrives in warm zones, the drier the better.

SEA KALE

Crambe maritima

Hardiness:
Zones 4–9

Shape:
Rosette

Color:
Blue leaf

Texture:
Bold, soft

Light:
Full sun

Size:
2–3 ft. high and wide

Character:
Medium herbaceous perennial grown for bold texture, rosette shape, white summer flower, multiseason bold foliage

A cousin of edible kale, sea kale settles into the garden as a bold rosette of ruffly, steel blue foliage. It prefers droughty soils with good drainage, and it's hardy to Zone 4. In early summer, it's topped by bouquets of dainty white flowers on long antennae-like arms that radiate from its center.

ACANTHUS

Acanthus species and cultivars

Hardiness: **Zones 5–10**	Texture: **Bold, glossy**
Shape: **Spiky rosette**	Light: **Full sun to part shade**
Color: **White and blue or purple flower**	Size: **3–4 ft. high, 2–4 ft. wide**

Character:
**Large herbaceous perennial grown
for white or blue summer flower, bold
texture, spiky rosette shape**

Known for their leaf and flower, hardy acanthus are large rosettes of ultra-glossy, mottled leaves. Towers of flower rise dramatically each summer. *Acanthus mollis* (Zone 7) has purple and white flowers, while prickly, hardier *A. spinosus* (Zone 5) trends toward blue.

AGAVE

FALSE ALOE

Manfreda virginica and cultivars and hybrids

Hardiness: **Zones (5–)7–10**	Texture: **Bold, soft**
Shape: **Spiky rosette**	Light: **Full sun**
Color: **Green or red-spotted leaf in cultivar**	Size: **3–5 ft. high, 3–4 ft. wide**

Character:
Medium herbaceous perennial grown for bold texture, spiky rosette shape, green flower

A drought-tolerant native of the Southeast, false aloe is an all-star for rocky soils, its fleshy rosettes multiply to form colonies, and in summer, each one throws up an eye-popping 4- to 5-foot spike of odd green flowers. *Manfreda* 'Spot' (pictured), a hybrid between *M. virginica* and *M. maculosa*, rates less hardy (Zone 7), but its leaves are speckled in burgundy.

• • • • • • • • • • • • • • • • • • •

ASTILBE

Astilbe cultivars

🌡	Hardiness:	**Zones 4–9**
🌿	Shape (flower):	**Plume**
🔌	Color:	**Red, pink, purple, or white flower**
#	Texture:	**Fine, soft**
☀	Light:	**Light shade to full shade**
📏	Size:	**12–36 in. high, 12–24 in. wide**

Character:

Small or medium herbaceous perennial grown for summer flower in various colors

A much-loved perennial for shade, lacy astilbe (pron. ah-still-BEE) is a quiet kid that thrives in cool, moist, wooded corners of gardens. In summer, it sends up soft, feathery plumes of bloom. Toughness varies between cultivars, but none, as a rule, enjoy excess heat, drought, or sun, and that is a problem.

PRAIRIE SMOKE

Geum triflorum

Hardiness:
Zones 3–7

Shape (flower):
Daisy to plume (in seed)

Color:
Pink flower, blue-green leaf

Texture:
Fine, soft

Light:
Full sun

Size:
6–12 in. high and wide

Character:

Small herbaceous perennial grown for pink spring fruit, pink spring flower, as groundcover

Prairie smoke gets its name from downy pink seedheads that hover above plants after they bloom, but this prairie native proves anything but delicate: it grows best in hot sun and lean soil. A fine coating of down covers its bluish leaves, too. Prairie smoke likes good drainage.

ASTILBE

GOATSBEARD / DWARF GOATSBEARD

Aruncus dioicus / Aruncus aethusifolius

Hardiness:
Zones 4–8

Shape (flower):
Plume

Color:
White flower

Texture:
Fine, soft

Light:
Full sun to part shade

Size:
1–6 ft. high, 1–4 ft. wide

Character:
Small to large herbaceous perennial grown for white summer flower

An old-fashioned native beloved by gardeners, goatsbeard (*Aruncus dioicus*) grows tall, and blooms with airy feathers of white in summer. Its small, nonnative cousin, *A. aethusifolius*, and its cultivars make for good edging plants. Both like damp soil, but adapt well to average or moderately dry conditions.

FLEECE FLOWER

Persicaria affinis **and cultivars**

Hardiness: **Zones (3–)5–9**	Texture: **Fine, soft**
Shape (flower): **Spike**	Light: **Full sun to light shade**
Color: **Pink flower, red fall leaf**	Size: **6 in. high, indefinite spread**

Character:
Small herbaceous perennial grown for pink multiseason flower; as groundcover

This fleece flower sports dainty pink spikes of flowers spring until fall, when it switches to red foliage. Once established, it's good with moisture or periods of drought, and takes sun in its upper range. Give it good drainage and a little shade in the heat of the day.

• • • • • • • • • • • • • • • • • •

BABY'S BREATH

Gypsophila paniculata and cultivars

🌡	Hardiness:	**Zones 3–9**
🌲	Shape (flower):	**Spray**
🖌	Color:	**White or pink flower**
###	Texture:	**Fine, soft**
☼	Light:	**Full sun**
📏	Size:	**2–3 ft. high and wide**

Character:
Small herbaceous perennial grown for pink or white multiseason flower, fine texture

Airy clumps of baby's breath play a supporting role in many a florists' bouquet. A fickle troublemaker, this plant won't stand for shade or wet feet, but in some parts of the United States where it grows readily, baby's breath is considered an invasive species.

'CHOCOLATE' SNAKEROOT

Ageratina altissima 'Chocolate'

🌡 🖌 ### ☼ 📏

Hardiness:
Zones 3–8

Shape (flower):
Bunch

Color:
White flower, purple leaf

Texture:
Medium in leaf, fine in flower, soft

Light:
Light shade to part shade

Size:
2–5 ft. high, 2–3 ft. wide

Character:
Medium herbaceous perennial grown for multiseason purple foliage, white fall flower

Native from the Rockies east, snakeroot blooms fluffy white in fall, and 'Chocolate' ups the ante with rich purple foliage all season. It colors up best with light shade. Plants may seed around, but flowers work well for cutting and for butterflies too. This cultivar is often sold as *Eupatorium rugosum* 'Chocolate'.

BOWMAN'S ROOT

Gillenia trifoliata

Hardiness: **Zones 4–8**	Texture: **Fine**
Shape (flower): **Spray**	Light: **Part sun to part shade**
Color: **Pink to white flower, red fall leaf**	Size: **2–4 ft. high, 1–3 ft. wide**

Character:
Medium herbaceous perennial grown for pink to white summer flower, fine texture

An underused eastern native, bowman's root explodes with sprays of delicate pink to white in summer. This adaptable beauty works well in all kinds of soils, both in shade and part sun. A woodland plant, it needs afternoon shade, but it's a straight A for dry shade once established. You may find it for sale as *Porteranthus trifoliatus*.

BABY'S BREATH

CALAMINT

Calamintha nepeta and cultivars

Hardiness:
Zones 5–10

Shape (flower):
Spray

Color:
White or lavender flower

Texture:
Fine

Light:
Full sun to part shade

Size:
1–2 ft. high and wide

Character:
Small herbaceous perennial grown for white or lavender fall flower, fine texture, fragrant multiseason foliage, as groundcover

Calamint and its cultivars bloom late summer to fall, with thousands of tiny white flowers peppered along upright branches. This fragrant-leaved mint relative makes great groundcover in sun or part shade. 'White Cloud' blooms most profusely, while 'Blue Cloud' blooms lavender.

BLEEDING HEART

Dicentra spectabilis

🌡	Hardiness:	**Zones 3–9**
	Shape (flower):	**Wand**
	Color:	**Pink or white flower**
	Texture:	**Bold to medium**
	Light:	**Part shade to full shade**
	Size:	**2–3 ft. high and wide**

Character:
Medium to large herbaceous perennial grown for pink or white spring flower

Bleeding heart is beloved for its teardrop pendants of bloom in late spring. But like a fickle paramour, it's ephemeral in all but the coolest parts of its range, retreating into the ground when summer heats up. Bleeding heart needs shade and won't tolerate drought.

BIGROOT GERANIUM

Geranium macrorrhizum

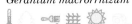

Hardiness:
Zones 5–10

Shape (flower):
Daisy

Color:
Pink or white flower

Texture:
Medium

Light:
Full sun to part shade

Size:
9–12 in. high, 18–24 in. wide

Character:
Small herbaceous perennial grown for pink or white spring flower, as groundcover

Bigroot geranium thrives even in dry shade, withstands humid climates, and takes part sun. While this vigorous beauty blooms in spring, its foliage looks great all season. 'Bevan's Variety' (pictured) blooms pink, 'Ingwersen's Variety' pink to white. For even tidier plants, shear foliage after flowering for a new flush.

BLEEDING HEART

GAURA

Gaura lindheimeri cultivars

Hardiness:
Zones 6–10

Shape (flower):
Wand

Color:
Pink or white flower

Texture:
Fine

Light:
Full sun to part shade

Size:
2–3 ft. high, 3–4 ft. wide

Character:
Small to medium herbaceous perennial grown for pink or white summer flower, fine texture

Gaura dances in summer with wands of flowers in shades of pink to white, and this southern native welcomes heat and humidity. It also takes drought, likes good drainage, and seeds around in ideal growing conditions. Gaura may flop in rich soils; try it on gentle slopes with small perennials and grasses for support, or look for compact cultivars.

FAIRY WAND

Dierama pulcherimmum

Hardiness:
Zones 7–10

Texture:
Fine to medium

Shape (flower):
Wand

Light:
Full sun

Color:
Pink to purple flower

Size:
3–6 ft. high, 3–4 ft. wide

Character:
Medium to large herbaceous perennial grown for pink summer flower, fine texture

Magically named fairy wand blooms late spring to summer with long stalks of bright, dangly flowers, and this easy plant's hummocky clump of leaves masquerades as an ornamental grass the rest of the season. All-star fairy wand is a snap in full sun and average soil.

CANNA

Canna cultivars

	Hardiness:	**Zones 7–10**
	Shape:	**Upright, paddle**
	Color:	**Red, pink, orange, yellow, or white flower, green, gold, or purple leaf**
	Texture:	**Bold**
	Light:	**Full sun**
	Size:	**2–8 ft. tall, 2–6 ft. wide**

Character:
Large herbaceous perennial grownfor summer flower in various colors, bold texture, multiseason foliage in various colors

Canna can definitely be a drama queen, its foliage fabulous one day, its flowers a hot mess the next. A raft of banana-like leaves punctuated by a topknot of floppy flowers, its foliage comes in an array of bodacious colors, and it's only hardy to Zone 7.

MILKWEED

Asclepias syriaca / Asclepias speciosa

Hardiness:	Texture:
Zones 4–9	**Bold**
Shape:	Light:
Upright, paddle	**Full sun**
Color:	Size:
Pink flower, green to silver-blue leaf	**2–4 ft. high, 1–3 ft. wide**

Character:
Medium herbaceous perennial grown for pink summer flower, bold texture

Famed as food for the monarch butterfly caterpillar, native milkweed proves a hardy, hearty low-water perennial, with big, lustrous leaves and fragrant flowers of pale pink. *Asclepias syriaca* is the eastern native, *A. speciosa* (pictured) out West. Plants can be allowed to colonize or kept in check by snapping off seed pods and runners.

CANNA

VARIEGATED FLEECE FLOWER

Persicaria amplexicaulis 'Golden Arrow' / *Persicaria microcephala* 'Red Dragon'

Hardiness:
Zones 4–9

Shape:
Branching, paddle

Color:
Pink or white flower, gold or purple leaf

Texture:
Bold

Light:
Part sun to part shade

Size:
2–6 ft. high and wide

Character:
Medium to large herbaceous perennial grown for multiseason gold or purple foliage, pink or white summer flower, bold texture

Cold-hardy with bold foliage, 'Golden Arrow' fleece flower comes in bright chartreuse-yellow, 'Red Dragon' (pictured) in deep maroon. The former needs room and blooms fuchsia in summer; the latter is more refined and heat-tolerant, happy as far south as Zone 9. Both prefer afternoon shade and average to moist soil.

216

ELECAMPANE

Inula magnifica

Hardiness:	Light:
Zones 5–9	**Full sun to light shade**
Shape:	
Upright, paddle	Size:
Color:	**4–8 ft. high, 3–5 ft. wide**
Gold flower	
Texture:	
Bold	

Character:
Large herbaceous perennial grown for bold texture, yellow summer flower, size

In the world of perennials with presence, elecampane is a towering inferno. This hardy plant's gigantic leaves and bold, gold summer daisies belie the fact it plays well with other garden plants, given the space. Give elecampane mostly sun and average garden conditions, sit back, and watch it grow.

CHRYSANTHEMUM

Chrysanthemum cultivars

🌡	Hardiness:	**Zones 5–9**
🌳	Shape:	**Mounded**
🎨	Color:	**Red, pink, orange, yellow, lavender, or white flower**
▦	Texture:	**Medium to bold**
☼	Light:	**Full sun**
📏	Size:	**18–30 in. tall and wide**

Character:
Small to medium herbaceous perennial grown for fall flower in various colors, mounded shape

Mums are bright, trendy kids who strike a pose in fall. Though they're perennials, mums most often get sent to the compost heap when winter comes. If kept on in the garden, most require plenty of pinching to remind them to be cute and compact, as well as fertilizer, and many still succumb to winter's chill.

PURPLE CONEFLOWER

Echinacea purpurea and cultivars

Hardiness: **Zones (4)5–9**	Texture: **Medium to bold**
Shape: **Upright**	Light: **Full sun**
Color: **Red, orange, pink, lavender, or white flower**	Size: **2–3 ft. high and wide**

Character:
Medium herbaceous perennial grown for summer flower in various colors

Native favorite echinaceas party hardy from mid to late summer, their pompons of bloom extending the show as they dry. An exciting group of newcomers, double-flowered cultivar 'Southern Belle' (pictured) is pretty in pink, 'Milkshake' comes in white, and 'Hot Papaya', a raucous red-orange. Plant these cones in well-drained soil in spring to get their roots established.

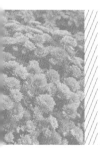

CHRYSAN-THEMUM

ASTER

Symphyotrichum novae-angliae 'Purple Dome' / *Symphyotrichum ×dumosus* cultivars

Hardiness:
Zones 5–8

Shape:
Mounded

Color:
**Pink or
purple flower**

Texture:
Medium to fine

Light:
**Full sun to
part shade**

Size:
**18–24 in. high,
18–36 in. wide**

Character:
**Small to medium herbaceous
perennial grown for pink or purple
fall flower, mounded shape**

Asters make outstanding garden additions, and a few cultivars are naturally tidy and bring a refreshing flush of pinks and purples to the garden in fall. 'Purple Dome' (pictured) is a blue-violet cultivar of native New England aster, while hybrids 'Wood's Pink' and 'Wood's Purple' round out the palette.

CUSHION SPURGE

Euphorbia polychroma and cultivars

Hardiness: **Zones 4–10**	Texture: **Medium to bold**
Shape: **Mounded**	Light: **Full sun**
Color: **Gold flower, gold, red, or purple leaf in cultivars**	Size: **12–24 in. high and wide**

Character:
Small to medium herbaceous perennial grown for gold spring flower, multiseason foliage in various colors in cultivars, mounded shape

Sometimes bright globes of bloom are called for in other seasons besides fall. Cushion spurge makes a hardy, drought-tolerant spring spectacular of fiery yellow flowers, and its colored foliage cultivars keep things interesting all season long. 'First Blush' has white-edged leaves, while 'Bonfire' boasts red.

DAYLILY

Hemerocallis species and cultivars

	Hardiness:	**Zones 3–9**
	Shape (flower):	**Trumpet**
	Color:	**Red, pink, orange, yellow, purple, or white flower**
	Texture:	**Bold in flower, medium in leaf**
	Light:	**Full sun to part shade**
	Size:	**1–4 ft. high and wide**

Character:
Small to medium herbaceous perennial grown for multiseason flower in various colors

Daylilies can be such a tease. These familiar plants bloom with bright trumpets on long stems off and on throughout the season, but each flower lasts just around a day. Like lots of overpopular plants, daylilies often present as blasé, especially their strappy leaves when they're not in bloom.

VARIEGATED DAYLILY

Hemerocallis 'Kwanso Variegata'
Hemerocallis 'Golden Zebra'

Hardiness:	**Zones 3–8**	Texture:	**Bold in flower, medium in leaf**
Shape (flower):	**Trumpet**	Light:	**Full sun to part shade**
Color:	**Yellow or orange flower, white-variegated leaf**	Size:	**1–4 ft. high and wide**

Character:
Small to medium herbaceous perennial grown for multiseason variegated foliage, yellow or orange summer flower

And now for a daylily that's completely different: one with fabulous foliage. In addition to bloom, several varieties show off with white-edged leaves—a treat throughout the growing season. 'Kwanso Variegata' blooms orange, and dwarf 'Golden Zebra' in gold. Give these cultivars afternoon shade.

ALSTROEMERIA

Alstroemeria hardy cultivars

Hardiness:
Zones 5–10

Shape (flower):
Trumpet

Color:
Red, pink, orange, yellow, purple, or white flower

Texture:
Fine to medium

Light:
Full sun to part shade

Size:
1–3 ft. high, 1–2 ft. wide

Character:
Small herbaceous perennial grown for summer flower in various colors

Alstroemeria blooms in summer with bright trumpets that last up to two weeks as cut flowers. Some alstros spread aggressively. A few hardy, well-behaved varieties include 'Mauve Majesty' (Zone 5, pictured), and 'Tangerine Tango' and 'Freedom' (Zone 6). Fragrant 'Sweet Laura' also shines in Zone 5, though she's a mover and shaker. Afternoon shade works best.

DAYLILY

CRINUM

Crinum cultivars

Hardiness:
Zones (5–)7–10

Shape (flower):
Trumpet

Color:
Pink or white flower

Texture:
Bold, glossy

Light:
Full sun to part shade

Size:
2–3 ft. high and wide

Character:
Medium perennial bulb grown for fragrant pink or white summer flower

An old-fashioned plant overdue for revival, crinum blooms white to pink in early to mid-summer, and these blushing beauties withstand conditions ranging from drought to standing water. Crinum thrives in warm climates, but with protection and dry winters, some, like the species *Crinum bulbispermum*, survive as far north as Zone 5.

DELPHINIUM

Delphinium species and cultivars

	Hardiness:	**Zones 3–10**
	Shape:	**Spike**
	Color:	**Blue flower**
	Texture:	**Medium to bold**
	Light:	**Full sun**
	Size:	**2–7 ft. high, 1–4 ft. wide**

Character:
Medium to large herbaceous perennial grown for blue summer flower, spike shape

With its cerulean tower of flower, delphinium entices all who aspire to the English cottage garden style. Alas, diva delph may be short-lived even if its demands for supplemental water and staking are met. It suffers in hot, humid climates and too often falls prey to pests and powdery mildew.

'BLUE FORTUNE' ANISE HYSSOP

Agastache 'Blue Fortune'

Hardiness:	**Zones 5–10**
Shape (flower):	**Spike**
Color:	**Blue-lavender flower**
Texture:	**Medium, soft**
Light:	**Full sun to light shade**
Size:	**2–3 ft. high and wide**

Character:
Medium herbaceous perennial grown for blue-lavender summer flower, fragrant multiseason foliage

'Blue Fortune' blooms in summer with scores of sea blue spires atop clean, minty foliage—convenient for butterflies. Its anise-scented leaves are great as garnishes and in teas. Low-water anise hyssops aren't wild about wet winters, but 'Blue Fortune' grows as well in New England as New Mexico.

DELPHINIUM

FOOTHILL PENSTEMON

Penstemon heterophyllus cultivars

Hardiness:
Zones 6–10

Shape (flower):
Spike

Color:
Blue flower

Texture:
Medium to fine

Light:
Full sun

Size:
**18 in. high
and wide**

Character:
**Small herbaceous perennial grown
for blue summer flower**

This tough, low-water plant's vivid blue spikes make it a must-have for gardeners who love "the blues." It blooms spring to summer, likes good drainage, and comes in several fantastic varieties. 'Blue Springs' (pictured) and 'Electric Blue' are like the sky on a clear day; 'Margarita BOP' fades from blue to lavender.

PRINCESS FLOWER

Tibouchina heteromalla

Hardiness: **Zones (8b)9–10**	Texture: **Bold, soft**
Shape (flower): **Daisy or spike**	Light: **Full sun**
Color: **Blue-purple flower**	Size: **6–15 ft. high and wide**

Character:
Medium to large evergreen shrub, flower

Princess flower blooms in the wildest blue-purple, and this species is most striking with silvery leaves and loosely vertical bouquets of bloom. This tender beauty dislikes frost, but other members of the *Tibouchina* clan grow as dieback perennials in Zone 8b. It's worth a shot for adventurous gardeners there.

227

DUSTY MILLER

Senecio cineraria

🌡	Hardiness:	**Zones 6–10**
🌿	Shape:	**Upright, feather**
🖌	Color:	**Silver leaf**
▦	Texture:	**Medium to fine, soft**
☼	Light:	**Full sun to part shade**
📏	Size:	**6–18 in. tall, 6–12 in. wide**

Character:
Small herbaceous perennial grown for multiseason silver foliage

Dusty miller is a classroom cheater—a silver-leaved perennial masquerading as an annual. Typically planted with the intention that it will be ripped out and replaced with something fresh the next year, too often it's forgotten, so it lingers, leggy and floppy, year after year.

MOUNTAIN MINT

Pycnanthemum muticum

Hardiness:
Zones 3–9

Shape:
Upright, mounded

Color:
Silver flower

Texture:
Medium, soft

Light:
Full sun to part shade

Size:
30–36 in. high, 18–24 in. wide

Character:
Medium herbaceous perennial, color accent, fragrance

Lots of plants have silver leaves, but how many have nickels for flowers? Eastern native mountain mint blooms in late summer with winged coins of silver atop tall stems. A butterfly bonanza, this fragrant-leaved mint prefers afternoon shade and spreads by runners, though it's more modest than most mints.

'HELENE VON STEIN' LAMB'S EAR

Stachys byzantina 'Helene von Stein'

Hardiness: **Zones 4–9**	Light: **Full sun to part shade**
Shape: **Mounded clump**	Size: **6–12 in. high, 12–24 in. wide**
Color: **Silver leaf**	
Texture: **Medium to bold, soft**	

Character:
Small herbaceous perennial grown for multiseason silver foliage, as groundcover

Some popular plants live up to the hype, and lamb's ear is one. An easy foliage plant with velvety silver leaves, it makes a fantastic low-water addition to any well-drained border. The big leaves of adaptable 'Helene von Stein' hold up better than others in humid climates, but it thrives in drought, too. This cultivar is some-times sold as *Stachys byzantina* 'Big Ears'.

DUSTY MILLER

PARTRIDGE FEATHER

Tanacetum densum subsp. *amani*

Hardiness:
Zones 5–10

Shape:
Upright, feather

Color:
Silver leaf

Texture:
Fine, soft

Light:
Full sun to light shade

Size:
4–8 in. high, 12–18 in. wide

Character:
Small herbaceous perennial grown for multiseason silver foliage, as groundcover

Like sterling feathers from the ground, little partridge feather rolls out a carpet of fine foliage fit for a king. This plant adores dry, rocky sites, hot or cold, and returns year after year with little more maintenance than a shear of spent foliage before spring.

FERN

Athyrium filix-femina

- Hardiness: **Zones 4–9**
- Shape: **Feather**
- Color: **Green leaf**
- Texture: **Fine, soft**
- Light: **Part shade to full shade**
- Size: **1–3 ft. high and wide**

Character:
Medium herbaceous perenial grown for fine texture, as groundcover

This particular fern, called lady fern, is the typically prissy kind: a stout clump of lacy fronds that unfurl from a central crown; it adores shade and grows in soil that's rich and preferably damp. Like many ferns, this lady takes a little dry shade, not true drought, and puts up with sun only with consistently moist soil.

SWEETFERN

Comptonia peregrina

Hardiness:
Zones 2–6

Shape:
Feather

Color:
Green leaf

Texture:
Fine, glossy

Light:
Full sun to part shade

Size:
2–4 ft. high, 4–8 ft. wide

Character:
Small deciduous shrub grown for fine texture, fragrant multiseason foliage, as groundcover

Like a fern from an alternate universe, native sweetfern thrives in poor, rocky soils of the East, in blazing sun or shade. This small shrub's ferny foliage smells beguilingly of citrus. Best transplanted from pot-grown stock, this anti-fern adapts to wet and dry conditions, excels in problem sites, and expands politely to form colonies once it settles in.

FERN

YARROW

Achillea species and cultivars

Hardiness:
Zones 3–8

Shape:
Feather

Color:
Red, orange, or yellow flower; green or silver leaf

Texture:
Fine

Light:
Full sun

Size:
2–4 ft. high and wide

Character:
Small to medium herbaceous perennial grown for summer flower in various colors, fine texture, as groundcover

A cottage garden mainstay, low-water yarrow thrives in full sun. Best known for bunch-shaped summer flowers in array of warm colors, it's overlooked for its beautiful, delicate foliage, attractive throughout the growing season. 'Coronation Gold' and 'Anthea' (pictured) are two tidy varieties that do well in all kinds of climates.

PALM SEDGE

Carex muskingumensis and cultivars

Hardiness:	Texture:
Zones 4–9	**Fine, glossy**
Shape:	Light:
Spiky, mounded	**Full sun to**
Color:	**part shade**
Green or gold-	Size:
variegated leaf	**2–3 ft. high**
(cultivar)	**and wide**

Character:
**Small to medium herbaceous
perennial grown for fine texture,
multiseason variegated foliage in
cultivar, as groundcover**

Like a party favor in plant form, palm sedge
has whorls of strappy leaves that radiate from
central spikes. It grows naturally in sun and
wet soil, but takes to shade and average garden conditions with flying colors. A Midwest
native, its cultivars include gilded 'Oehme',
each of its leaves edged in gold.

• • • • • • • • • • • • • • • • •

233

FORGET-ME-NOT

Myosotis species

🌡	Hardiness:	**Zones 3–9**
🌲	Shape (flower):	**Spray**
🖌	Color:	**Blue flower**
▦	Texture:	**Medium to fine**
☼	Light:	**Full sun to part shade**
📏	Size:	**6–12 in. high and wide**

Character:
Small herbaceous perennial grown for blue spring flower, as groundcover

The seemingly innocent kid who spreads rumors behind your back, forget-me-not is best known for its sweet starbursts of true blue in spring. This charmer likes to grow where it's cool and wet, and sweet though it may be, it's an invasive species in woodlands and wetlands across North America.

VARIEGATED JACOB'S LADDER

Polemonium reptans 'Stairway to Heaven'

Hardiness: **Zones 4–9**	Texture: **Fine**
Shape (flower): **Bunch**	Light: **Part shade to full shade**
Color: **Blue flower, pink- to white-variegated leaf**	Size: **6–18 in. high, 12–18 in. wide**

Character:
Small herbaceous perennial grown for multiseason variegated foliage, blue summer flower, as groundcover

A cultivar of eastern native Jacob's ladder, 'Stairway to Heaven' is a tiny peacock that puts on a show all season. In early spring, green leaves emerge edged in pink, later fade to white to complement clear blue flowers, then turn yellow-green. 'Stairway' takes moderately dry shade once established.

**FORGET-
ME-NOT**

PLUMBAGO

Ceratostigma plumbaginoides

| | | | | | |

Hardiness:
Zones 5–9

Shape (flower):
Bunch

Color:
**Blue flower, red-
orange fall leaf**

Texture:
Medium to fine

Light:
**Full sun to
part shade**

Size:
**6–12 in. high,
12–18 in. wide**

Character:
**Small herbaceous perennial grown
for blue summer flower, as
groundcover, red-orange fall foliage**

A sensationally multifaceted plant, drought-
tolerant plumbago thrives in sun or shade in a
range of climates from coast to coast. It makes a
terrific groundcover, blooms opalescent blue in
summer, and follows that with an uncommon
bonus for a perennial: its leaves turn fiery red-
orange in fall.

BLUE-EYED MARY

Omphalodes cappadocica and cultivars

Hardiness: **Zones 6–9**	Texture: **Medium to fine**
Shape (flower): **Spray**	Light: **Part shade to full shade**
Color: **Blue flower**	Size: **6–18 in. high, 12–18 in. wide**

Character:
Small herbaceous perennial grown for blue spring flower

Blue-eyed Mary blooms with sprays of clear cerulean flowers in spring, and this shady beauty brightens dim corners with just as much vigor in damp shade or dry. 'Starry Eyes' features blue flowers intricately edged in faded pink, turning to white.

● ● ● ● ● ● ● ● ● ● ● ● ● ● ● ● ●

FOXGLOVE

Digitalis purpurea and cultivars

	Hardiness:	**Zones 4–8**
	Shape (flower):	**Spike**
	Color:	**Pink to peach or yellow flower**
	Texture:	**Bold, soft**
	Light:	**Full sun to part shade**
	Size:	**2–7 ft. high, 1–4 ft. wide**

Character:
Medium to large herbaceous perennial or biennial grown for summer flower in various colors, spike shape

In the pickup game in the school-yard of plants, foxglove would be best at fake-outs. A biennial, it grows its first year, blooms and sets seed the second, and may not return after that. It prefers rich soil of moderate moisture, though not wet, and its looks tend to slide a bit after it blooms.

GAS PLANT

Dictamnus albus

Hardiness:
Zones 3–9

Shape (flower):
Spike

Color:
Pink or white flower

Texture:
Bold, glossy

Light:
Full sun to light shade

Size:
2–5 ft. high, 1–2 ft. wide

Character:
Medium to large herbaceous perennial grown for pink or white summer flower, spike shape

A linebacker among perennials, long-lived gas plant sparkles with pink or pinkish-white spires in early summer. Its dark green, bushy foliage gives it presence year-round. This tap-rooted perennial doesn't catch its stride until it's in the ground, but give it time. Citrusy oils from crushed leaves can irritate skin.

CAROLINA LUPINE

Thermopsis caroliniana

Hardiness:
Zones 3–9

Shape (flower):
Spike

Color:
Yellow flower

Texture:
Medium to bold, glossy

Light:
Full sun

Size:
3–5 ft. high, 3–4 ft. wide

Character:
Large herbaceous perennial grown for yellow summer flower, spike shape

Carolina lupine's name says it all: this deep-rooted native of the sultry Southeast takes heat, drought, and humidity, blooms with spires of canary yellow flowers in early summer, and its tidy trefoil foliage stays crisp into fall.

239

FOXGLOVE

MULLEIN

Verbascum species and cultivars

Hardiness:	Texture:
Zones 5–10	**Bold**

Shape (flower):	Light:
Spike	**Full sun**

Color:	Size:
Yellow, pink, peach, or white flower	**2–8 ft. high, 1–3 ft. wide**

Character:
Medium to large herbaceous perennial or biennial grown for summer flower in various colors, spike shape

Easy, elegant, and drought tolerant, mullein and its cultivars vary from giant *Verbascum olympicum* (pictured) to prim *V. chaixii*. Rebloomers like rose-pink 'Southern Charm' can be cut back to their rosettes after flowering for another round. Some mullein may be biennial, but most reseed enthusiastically, and many far outlast their two-year past-due date.

● ● ● ● ● ● ● ● ● ● ● ● ● ● ● ● ● ● ●

GLADIOLUS

Gladiolus cultivars

🌡	Hardiness:	**Zones 7–10**
	Shape (flower):	**Spike**
	Color:	**Pink, red, orange, yellow, purple, or white flower**
▦	Texture:	**Bold**
☼	Light:	**Full sun to light shade**
	Size:	**2–6 ft. high, 1–2 ft. wide**

Character:

Large perennial bulb grown for summer flower in various colors, spike shape

Gladiolus tries really hard to be cool, with its pointy green leaves and flowers like the ruffled shirt-fronts of vintage tuxedos. Try as it might, gangly glad's height means it often needs staking. It's only hardy to Zone 7, and even then may fall victim to the coldest winters and hottest summers.

BLAZING STAR

Liatris species and cultivars

Hardiness:
Zones 3–9

Shape (flower):
Spike

Color:
Pink or white flower

Texture:
Fine, glossy in leaf, soft in flower

Light:
Full sun

Size:
2–5 ft. high, 1–2 ft. wide

Character:
Medium herbaceous perennial grown for pink or white summer flower, spike shape

Native to most of North America, blazing star scores with pink spires in summer, great for cutting, and this hardy perennial adapts to a range of conditions. Favorites include *Liatris spicata* (pictured), with popular cultivars like compact 'Kobold' and white 'Alba', and taller *L. pycnostachya*, or prairie blazing star.

GLADIOLUS

HARDY GLADIOLUS

Gladiolus 'Boone' / *Gladiolus* 'Carolina Primrose' / *Gladiolus communis* subsp. *byzantinus*

Hardiness:	Texture:
Zones 5–8	**Bold**
Shape (Flower):	Light:
Spike	**Full sun**
Color:	Size:
Yellow, peach, or purple flower	**1–3 ft. high, 1–2 ft. wide**

Character:
Medium perennial bulb grown for multiseason flower in various colors, spike shape

Cold-hardy glads become more available at better retailers all the time, and these varieties tend to be tough and low maintenance. Midsummer to fall sees 'Boone' in apricot and yellow, 'Carolina Primrose' in pale yellow. Smaller *G. communis* subsp. *byzantinus* (pictured) blooms late spring in jewel-tone red-purple. Give them all great drainage and a winter mulch for good measure.

BUTTERFLY GINGER

Hedychium species and cultivars

Hardiness: **Zones 7b–10**	Character: **Large herbaceous perennial grown for summer flower in various colors, bold texture, multiseason variegated foliage in cultivars, spike shape**
Shape (Flower): **Spike**	
Color: **Red, pink, orange, yellow, or white flower**	

Texture:
Bold

Light:
Part sun to part shade

Size:
4–6 ft. high and wide

For shade and average to damp soils in warm climates, butterfly ginger dazzles with exotic foliage and tall spikes of fragrant summer flowers in a range of colors. It likes afternoon shade and dies back in winters with hard frost. Variegated 'Tahitian Flame' (pictured) and 'Doctor Moy' are the life of any tiki party.

• • • • • • • • • • • • • • • • • •

243

GOLDENROD

Solidago species

🌡	Hardiness:	**Zones 3–9**
🌲	Shape (flower):	**Bunch**
🌿	Color:	**Yellow flower**
▦	Texture:	**Medium to fine, soft**
☀	Light:	**Full sun to part shade**
📏	Size:	**2–4 ft. high and wide**

Character:
Medium to large herbaceous perennial grown for yellow fall flower, fine texture

Goldenrod is a good kid who hangs out with a bad crowd—that's why it's forever blamed for the misery of allergy sufferers everywhere. While the real culprit is ragweed (*Ambrosia* species), many gardeners still insist goldenrod makes them sneeze and would rather look to other plants for garden gold.

BUTTERFLY WEED

Asclepias tuberosa and cultivars

Hardiness: **Zones 3–10**	Texture: **Medium to bold**
Shape (flower): **Bunch**	Light: **Full sun**
Color: **Orange or yellow flower**	Size: **1–2 ft. high and wide**

Character:
Small to medium herbaceous perennial grown for orange or yellow summer flower

An easy, low-water perennial native to most of North America, butterfly weed fires off bouquets of bright orange all summer long. Like other milkweeds, this little plant is a lifeline to monarch butterfly larvae wherever it grows. Butterfly weed thrives in dry, sunny sites and shies away from wet soils.

GOLDENROD

RABBIT BRUSH

Ericameria nauseosa

Hardiness:
Zones 4–9

Shape (flower):
Bunch

Color:
Yellow flower

Texture:
Fine, soft

Light:
Full sun

Size:
**2–6 ft. high,
2–4 ft. wide**

Character:
**Medium deciduous shrub grown for
yellow fall flower, fine texture**

A traffic-stopping sign of fall to anyone in
the arid West, rabbit brush sets the desert landscape ablaze with crackling gold
garlands of bloom above blue-gray foliage.
These turn to fluffy seedheads birds adore,
then fade and dry for winter. Prune rabbit
brush in spring to keep it neat. It's often
sold as *Chrysothamnus nauseosus*.

GOLDEN LACE

Patrinia scabiosifolia

Hardiness:	Texture:
Zones 5–8	**Fine, soft**
Shape (flower):	Light:
Bunch	**Full sun to part shade**
Color:	
Yellow flower	Size:
	3–6 ft. high, 2–3 ft. wide

Character:
Large herbaceous perennial grown for yellow summer flower, fine texture

Golden lace is a shy charmer that blooms in a veil of cheery yellow bouquets atop tall stems over a long period in summer. This gossamer beauty grows best with afternoon shade. Give it average garden conditions otherwise, even damp soils, and golden lace thrives.

● ● ● ● ● ● ● ● ● ● ● ● ● ● ● ● ● ●

247

HOSTA

Hosta cultivars

🌡	Hardiness:	**Zones 3–9**
🌳	Shape:	**Mounded rosette**
✂	Color:	**Green, blue, gold, or white-variegated leaf**
▦	Texture:	**Bold**
☀	Light:	**Light shade to full shade**
📏	Size:	**1–4 ft. high and wide**

Character:
Small to large herbaceous perennial grown for bold texture, multiseason foliage in various colors, as groundcover

If one plant is the golden boy, hosta is that plant. It's the star quarterback, beloved by all, at the top of every class—almost. For all their great qualities, hostas don't do all-day hot sun and soil, they're especially beloved by big slugs, and let's face it: they're everywhere. Hard to come by, hostas aren't.

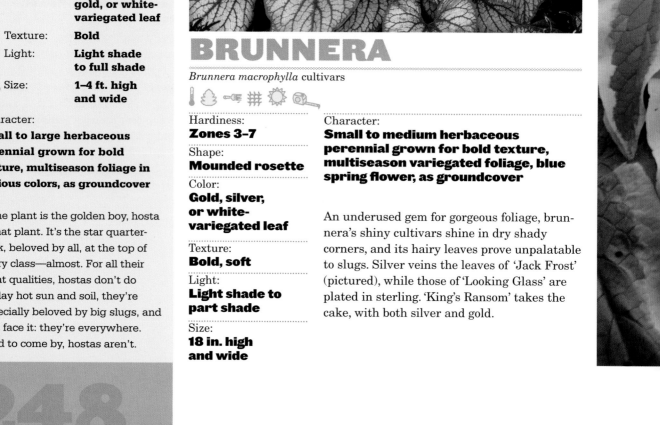

BRUNNERA

Brunnera macrophylla cultivars

🌡 🌳 ✂ ▦ ☀ 📏

Hardiness:
Zones 3–7

Shape:
Mounded rosette

Color:
Gold, silver, or white-variegated leaf

Texture:
Bold, soft

Light:
Light shade to part shade

Size:
18 in. high and wide

Character:
Small to medium herbaceous perennial grown for bold texture, multiseason variegated foliage, blue spring flower, as groundcover

An underused gem for gorgeous foliage, brunnera's shiny cultivars shine in dry shady corners, and its hairy leaves prove unpalatable to slugs. Silver veins the leaves of 'Jack Frost' (pictured), while those of 'Looking Glass' are plated in sterling. 'King's Ransom' takes the cake, with both silver and gold.

VARIEGATED COMFREY

Symphytum ×uplandincum 'Axminster Gold'

Hardiness: **Zones 4–9**	Texture: **Bold, soft**
Shape: **Mounded rosette**	Light: **Full sun to part shade**
Color: **Yellow-variegated leaf, pink flower**	Size: **3 ft. high and wide, flower up to 6 ft.**

Character:
Large herbaceous perennial grown for bold texture, multiseason variegated foliage, pink summer flower, as groundcover

You may know comfrey as an old-timey folk remedy, but today it's grown mostly for looks, and it doesn't get any better in foliage than 'Axminster Gold.' Colorful in sun or shade, its bold, gold-edged leaves make a statement in damp soil or dry. Chop 'Axminster' to the ground after it blooms for a new flush.

HOSTA

'LUNAR GLOW' BERGENIA

Bergenia 'Lunar Glow'

Hardiness:
Zones 4–9

Shape:
Upright, paddle

Color:
Yellow to red leaf, pink flower

Texture:
Bold, glossy

Light:
Part shade to full shade

Size:
1–2 ft. high and wide

Character:
Medium herbaceous perennial grown for bold texture, multiseason foliage in various colors, pink spring flower, as groundcover

An all-star in dry rock gardens as much as pondside, bergenia's big, shiny, cabbagey leaves are a treat year-round. 'Lunar Glow' adds a shot of color to the show. New leaves emerge yellow, turn first to green, then to spectacular wine red in fall. In mild climates, bergenia is evergreen.

• • • • • • • • • • • • • • • • • • • •

IRIS—BEARDED

Iris cultivars, bearded

🌡️	Hardiness:	**Zones 3–10**
🌿	Shape (flower):	**Fan**
🔌	Color:	**Red, pink, orange, yellow, blue, or purple flower**
▦	Texture:	**Bold**
☀️	Light:	**Full sun**
📐	Size:	**2–4 ft. high and wide**

Character:

Medium herbaceous perennial grown for fan-shaped summer flower in various colors

The best known iris on the block is bearded iris. These tough beauties bloom for a short period in early summer, but won't stand for too much shade or too little drainage, and need division every few years to keep blooming. Irises have unique flowers, like paper fans that float above sword-shaped leaves.

VARIEGATED IRIS

Iris pallida 'Variegata' / *Iris pallida* 'Argentea Variegata'

🌡️ 🌿 🔌 ▦ ☀️ 📐

Hardiness:
Zones 4–9

Shape (flower):
Fan

Color:
Lavender flower, white- or gold-variegated leaf

Texture:
Bold

Light:
Full sun

Size:
2–3 ft. high, 1–2 ft. wide

Character:

Medium herbaceous perennial grown for fan-shaped lavender summer flower; multiseason variegated foliage

Everybody grows bearded irises for flower, but what about irises for fabulous foliage all season? These two cultivars do bloom prettily with blue-lavender fans in early summer, but 'Variegata' truly shines for tiger-striped leaves, as does its sister 'Argentea Variegata' (pictured) in silver-white.

**IRIS—
BEARDED**

JAPANESE ROOF IRIS

Iris tectorum and cultivars

Hardiness:
Zones 4–9

Shape (flower):
Fan

Color:
**Blue and
white flower**

Texture:
Bold, glossy

Light:
**Full sun to
part shade**

Size:
**1–2 ft. high
and wide**

Character:
**Medium herbaceous perennial
grown for fan-shaped blue and white
summer flower**

Not only does roof Japanese iris bloom with an
ocean of blue fans in spring, it also raises the
roof with dark green, glossy leaves that grow in
rosettelike clumps and spread to form a super
foliage accent even when the plant isn't blooming. This iris takes more shade than others.

LOUISIANA IRIS

Iris cultivars, Louisiana iris types

Hardiness: **Zones 5–9**	Texture: **Bold**
Shape (flower): **Fan**	Light: **Full sun to part shade**
Color: **Red, pink, orange, yellow, blue, or purple flower**	Size: **2–3 ft. high, 1–2 ft. wide**

Character:
Medium herbaceous perennial grown for fan-shaped summer flower in various colors

An underrated all-star among irises for wet soils, Louisiana iris hales from the bayous and marshes of that and other southern states, but takes to average garden conditions in full sun to part shade as far north as Zone 5.

253

LAVENDER

Lavandula species

🌡	Hardiness:	**Zones 3–10**
☁	Shape (flower):	**Spike**
🔌	Color:	**Lavender-blue flower, silver leaf**
▦	Texture:	**Fine, soft**
☀	Light:	**Full sun**
📏	Size:	**2–4 ft. high and wide**

Character:
Small to medium herbaceous perennial grown for lavender-blue summer flower, fragrant year-round silver foliage, as hedge, as groundcover

Another bewitching exchange student who won't stick around, lavender craves sun, warmth, well-drained alkaline soil, and dry air. With care, some varieties will grow in cold and humid climates, but much of North American simply isn't to lavender's liking, nor is a damp or shady site.

HYSSOP

Hyssopus officinalis

Hardiness:
Zones 4–9

Shape (flower):
Spike

Color:
Pink or blue flower

Texture:
Fine, glossy

Light:
Full sun to part shade

Size:
18–24 in. high, 12–18 in. wide

Character:
Small to medium herbaceous perennial grown for pink or blue summer flower, fragrant multiseason foliage, as hedge

An underused aromatic gem for shrubby edging, hyssop grows easily in all but wet soils and readily adapts to partial shade, especially on hot, bright afternoons. A tough-as-nails trooper, hyssop takes drought once it's settled and asks only for well-drained soil. Light shearing in early summer keeps it tidy.

'WALKER'S LOW' CATMINT

Nepeta ×faassenii 'Walker's Low'

Hardiness:	Texture:
Zones 4–8	**Fine, soft**
Shape (flower):	Light:
Spike	**Full sun to part shade**
Color:	
Lavender flower	Size:
	2–3 ft. high and wide

Character:
Medium herbaceous perennial grown for lavender summer flower, fragrant multiseason silver foliage, as groundcover

Plant it in any average sunny space and stand back—'Walker's Low' will take it from there. This easy spreading catmint sends up blue-lavender spikes of bloom late spring that last for weeks, and smells of herb and cola to the touch. Give it well-drained soil, and afternoon shade in hot, humid climates.

LAVENDER

BLUEBEARD

Caryopteris ×clandonensis cultivars

Hardiness:
Zones 5–9

Shape (flower):
Spike

Color:
Blue flower, silver leaf

Texture:
Medium, soft

Light:
Full sun to part shade

Size:
2–4 ft. high and wide

Character:
Medium deciduous shrub grown for blue fall flower, multiseason silver foliage, as hedge

A cinch in average, well-drained soils, lemon-scented bluebeard thrives in sun or part shade, heat, and drought. True to its name, it's a late-summer sendoff in brilliant blue. Cut bluebeard to the ground in late winter to keep it neat. 'Longwood Blue' grows tall; 'Worcester Gold' has yellow foliage all season.

● ● ● ● ● ● ● ● ● ● ● ● ● ● ● ● ● ● ●

PEONY

Paeonia lactiflora cultivars

🌡	Hardiness:	**Zones 3–8**
🌿	Shape (flower):	**Cup, often double**
🔑	Color:	**Red, pink, yellow, purple, or white flower**
▦	Texture:	**Bold**
☼	Light:	**Full sun to part shade**
📏	Size:	**2–3 ft. high and wide**

Character:
Medium herbaceous perennial grown for spring flower in various colors

Peony blooms in spring with huge, homecoming corsage flowers. This queen typically needs winter cold to bloom, and it's tough in its preferred temperate climate, but droughty soils are so not peony's thing. Top-heavy flowers often tip over; plant peony too deeply, and you can forget flowers altogether.

HELLEBORE

Helleborus ×hybridus cultivars

Hardiness:
Zones 4–9

Shape (flower):
Cup, sometimes double

Color:
Pink, purple, or white flower

Texture:
Bold

Light:
Part shade to full shade

Size:
12–18 in. high and wide

Character:
Medium herbaceous perennial grown for late winter flower in various colors

Hope springs eternal with hellebore in late winter, when its delicate flower cups appear while the rest of the garden slumbers. In climates without heavy snow, hellebore's foliage carpets the ground year-round. Showy double-flowered varieties dazzle as cut flowers for small vases, or floated in bowls.

PEONY

PRICKLY PEAR

Opuntia species

Hardiness: **Zones 4–10**	Texture: **Bold**
Shape (flower): **Cup**	Light: **Full sun**
Color: **Pink, yellow, or white flower**	Size: **1–15 ft. high, 1–10 ft. wide**

Character:
Small to large evergreen succulent grown for bold texture, summer flower in various colors, as groundcover

Known for its classic cacti silhouette, prickly pear blooms spectacularly too, with gobs of glowing cups in warm colors. Species of this genus of low-water plants are native and hardy across North America. *Opuntia ellisiana* (Zones 6–10) is nearly prickle-free. Natives *O. humifusa* and *O. polyacantha* are hardy to Zone 4. All need only sun and well-drained soil, especially in climates with wet winters.

CONFEDERATE ROSE

Hibiscus mutabilis and cultivars

Hardiness:
Zones 7–10

Shape (flower):
Cup, sometimes double

Color:
Red, pink, or white flower

Texture:
Bold

Light:
Full sun to light shade

Size:
8–15 in. high, 6–10 in. wide

Character:
Large deciduous shrub grown for fall flower in various colors

The huge ruffly cups of confederate rose breathe life into mild-climate gardens in fall, when little else blooms: first they're white, then they age to pink, and finally deep rose. This big, low-water knockout maintains its shrubbiness in frost-free zones and dies all the way to the ground in winter above Zone 9.

· · · · · · · · · · · · · · · · · ·

PHLOX

Phlox paniculata cultivars

	Hardiness:	**Zones 3–7**
	Shape (flower):	**Bunch**
	Color:	**Red, pink, purple, or white flower**
	Texture:	**Medium in leaf, bold in flower**
	Light:	**Full sun**
	Size:	**2–4 ft. tall, 2–3 ft. wide**

Character:

Large herbaceous perennial grown for fragrant summer flower in various colors

When garden phlox is hot, it sparkles, its voluptuous drumsticks of fragrant flowers a tall, cool taste of summer. When it's not, it's an overplayed trend that's lost its luster—a floppy mess, the poster child for powdery mildew, especially in humid climates and damp soils.

DWARF JOE PYE WEED

Eupatorium dubium 'Little Joe'

Hardiness:	**Zones 3–9**	Light:	**Full sun to light shade**
Shape (flower):	**Bunch**	Size:	**3–4 ft. high, 2–3 ft. wide**
Color:	**Pink flower**		
Texture:	**Medium in leaf, bold in flower**		

Character:

Medium to large herbaceous perennial grown for fragrant pink summer flower

Wherever native Joe Pye weed blooms, butterflies are sure to follow, and so it goes with dwarf 'Little Joe.' This little Joe that could bursts into bloom with fragrant, fuzzy clubs of butterfly-beloved pink in midsummer. It's an easy, low-water plant, and thrives both in wet soils and dry. It may also be sold as *Eupatoriadelphus dubius* 'Little Joe'.

NEW YORK IRONWEED

Vernonia noveboracensis

Hardiness:
Zones 5–9

Shape (flower):
Bunch

Color:
Purple flower

Texture:
Medium to fine

Light:
Full sun

Size:
**4–7 ft. high,
2–4 ft. wide**

Character:
**Large herbaceous perennial grown
for purple fall flower**

Ironweed's fall flowers twinkle like purple
stars atop stout stems. This adaptable,
drought-tolerant eastern native grows just as
happily in wetlands as dry roadsides. If its
height is an issue, cut new stems to the ground
in late spring for shorter plants. Ironweed will
seed around if it's in the right spot.

PHLOX

'MATRONA' SEDUM

Sedum 'Matrona'

Hardiness:
Zones 3–10

Shape (flower):
Bunch

Color:
**White to pink
to red flower**

Texture:
**Medium to
bold, soft**

Light:
**Full sun to
light shade**

Size:
**2–3 ft. high
and wide**

Character:
**Medium herbaceous perennial grown
for multiseason flower in various
colors, bold texture**

Flowers of 'Matrona' sedum start as white drumsticks in high summer, mature gradually to pink, darken to red by fall, and turn chestnut brown in winter until they're cleaned up for spring. As if that weren't enough, this succulent, low-water showoff sports steely blue leaves and red stems all season long. It is sometimes sold as *Hylotelephium* 'Matrona'.

• • • • • • • • • • • • • • • • • •

POPPY

Papaver orientale cultivars

	Hardiness:	**Zones 3–7**
	Shape (flower):	**Cup**
	Color:	**Red, pink, orange, yellow, or white flower**
	Texture:	**Medium to bold**
	Light:	**Full sun**
	Size:	**12–36 in. high, 18–24 in. wide**

Character:

Medium herbaceous perennial grown for spring flower in various colors

A vision of translucent petals in late spring, Oriental poppy is the flighty hippie chick with strict dietary requirements. It founders in climates with mild winters, and where it grows well, this poppy won't stand for wet, poorly drained soil or too much shade, often needs staking, and plays dormant in summer.

WINE CUPS

Callirhoe involucrata

Hardiness:
Zones 4–9

Shape (flower):
Cup

Color:
Pink-purple flower

Texture:
Medium to fine

Light:
Full sun

Size:
6–12 in. high, 12–36 in. wide

Character:

Small herbaceous perennial grown for pink-purple multiseason flower, as groundcover

Wine cups blooms in a glowing shade of rose all throughout the growing season. This low-water poppy cousin takes heat and drought, and politely weaves itself in among larger plants. Give it sun and good drainage, and this rugged little plant will thrive in climes of all kinds.

CELANDINE POPPY

Stylophorum diphyllum

Hardiness:
Zones 4–9

Shape (flower):
Cup

Color:
Yellow flower

Texture:
Medium

Light:
Part shade to full shade

Size:
12–18 in. high and wide

Character:
Medium herbaceous perennial grown for yellow spring flower

Celandine poppy sparkles with yellow spring flowers and silvery leaves. While this eastern native likes damp woodlands, it thrives even in moderately dry shade. Celandine goes summer dormant with excess drought, but it brings a fresh foliar flush with fall rains. This poppy seeds around in the right growing conditions.

POPPY

SPANISH POPPY

Papaver atlanticum and cultivars

Hardiness:
Zones 5–10

Shape (flower):
Cup

Color:
Orange flower

Texture:
Medium to fine, soft

Light:
Full sun to light shade

Size:
8–12 in. high, 10–12 in. wide

Character:
Small herbaceous perennial grown for orange multiseason flower

Another low-water plant with a long season, Spanish poppy begins to bloom in late spring and keeps it up well through summer, supported by showy silvery blue-green foliage in the meantime. At home in any well-drained soil, it may be short-lived, but spreads politely by seed. 'Flore Pleno' is a double delight.

PRICKLY PEAR

Opuntia ficus-indica

🌡	Hardiness:	**Zones 9–11**
🪴	Shape:	**Rounded pad**
🎨	Color:	**Red, yellow, or white flower**
▦	Texture:	**Bold**
☀	Light:	**Full sun**
📏	Size:	**8–15 ft. tall, 8–10 ft. wide**

Character:
Medium to large evergreen succulent grown for bold texture, summer flower in various colors, edible summer fruit, as groundcover

The humble cactus is a desert icon, and this particular prickly pear is iconic among cacti as a food crop. It's a tough customer that adores heat, drought, and lean, fast-draining soil. This pear, however, is all bark and no bite: its tender pads can't endure the freeze/thaw cycles of wet winter zones.

EASTERN PRICKLY PEAR

Opuntia humifusa

🌡 🪴 🎨 ▦ ☀

Hardiness:	**Zones 4–10**
Shape:	**Rounded pad**
Color:	**Yellow flower**
Texture:	**Bold**
Light:	**Full sun**
Size:	**8–14 in. high, 12–18 in. wide**

Character:
Small evergreen succulent grown for bold texture, yellow summer flower, edible summer fruit, as groundcover

One native cactus calls the entire eastern half of North America home, from New England to the South. A little plant with a lot of character, eastern prickly pear enjoys sun and rocky, sandy soil, sports buttery yellow flowers and edible fruit, and grows well with good drainage even in cold, humid climates.

PRICKLY PEAR

PLAINS PRICKLY PEAR

Opuntia polyacantha cultivars

Hardiness:
Zones 4–10

Shape:
Rounded pad

Color:
Pink, yellow, or white flower

Texture:
Bold

Light:
Full sun

Size:
4–8 in. high, 12–18 in. wide

Character:
Small evergreen succulent grown for bold texture, summer flower in various colors, edible summer fruit, as groundcover

Another native cactus, plains prickly pear makes its home on arid sites of the Great Plains. As a plant of that region, it handles wet winters as well, and this adorably spiny cactus comes in an array of varieties for flower. Its fruit is edible too.

TREE CHOLLA

Cylindropuntia imbricata cultivars

Hardiness: **Zones 5–10**	Texture: **Bold**
Shape: **Upright, branching**	Light: **Full sun**
Color: **Pink flower**	Size: **2–8 ft. high, 2–3 ft. wide**

Character:
**Medium to large evergreen
succulent grown for bold texture,
pink summer flower**

An awesomely prickly plant, tree cholla hales
from hot and cold arid regions of the West,
flowers in purply-pink, and branches out
to form picturesque "trees." Cholla will be
smaller and its "arms" may slouch in wet-
winter climates, but with well-drained soil, it
grows well and blooms cheerfully.

PRIMROSE

Primula species and cultivars

🌡	Hardiness:	**Zones 3–9**
🌲	Shape (flower):	**Bunch**
🖌	Color:	**Red, pink, yellow, blue, purple, or white flower**
▦	Texture:	**Medium to bold, soft**
☼	Light:	**Light shade to full shade**
📏	Size:	**12–18 in. tall, 8–12 in. wide**

Character:
Small herbaceous perennial grown for spring flower in various colors, as groundcover

Primroses greet the growing season in spring with bouquets of pastel-colored cups and ruffled foliage. True to their name, these prim, temperate beauties shy away from sun and hot climates, both dry and humid. Moist, cool soil and shade are a must for most primroses.

BERGENIA

Bergenia cordifolia and cultivars

Hardiness:	Texture:
Zones 3–8	**Bold, glossy**
Shape (flower):	Light:
Bunch	**Part shade to full shade**
Color:	
Pink to white flower	Size:
	1–2 ft. high and wide

Character:
Medium herbaceous perennial grown for bold texture, pink to white spring flower; as groundcover

Usually grown for foliage, bergenia shows off in bloom too, with delicate pink-white bundles of bells—though its plump, waxy leaves do keep things interesting all season. Give bergenia shade and it thrives in wet or dry. In mild climates it's evergreen, and leaves turn red-purple in winter.

PRIMROSE

FOAMFLOWER

Tiarella cordifolia and cultivars

Hardiness:
Zones 4–9

Shape (flower):
Spike

Color:
**Pink to
white flower**

Texture:
**Medium to
fine, soft**

Light:
**Full sun to
part shade**

Size:
**6–12 in. high
and wide**

Character:
**Small herbaceous perennial grown
for pink to white summer flower; fine
texture, as groundcover**

An eastern native, foamflower sends up spikes
of pink to white flowers in early summer and
grows with gusto in wet or dry shade. This
little champ spreads by runners and makes a
great groundcover. Many cultivars grow tapestries of intricately patterned all-season foliage.

BRIDAL WREATH

Francoa sonchifolia and cultivars

Hardiness:
Zones 7–9

Shape (flower):
Spike

Color:
Pink or white flower

Texture:
Medium to bold in leaf, glossy, fine in flower

Light:
Light shade to part shade

Size:
18–36 in. high, 12–18 in. wide

Character:
Medium herbaceous perennial grown for pink or white summer flower, fine texture, as groundcover

Don't let its name fool you: bridal wreath is an all-star and a breath of fresh air for damp or dry shade. In mid to late summer, its tall, slender flower spikes float vertically above clumps of evergreen, cabbage-patch leaves. The species blooms white, while shorter 'Rogerson's Form' is magenta.

● ● ● ● ● ● ● ● ● ● ● ● ● ● ● ● ●

273

YUCCA

Yucca filamentosa

🌡	Hardiness:	**Zones 5–10**
🌲	Shape:	**Spiky rosette**
🖌	Color:	**Blue-green leaf, white flower**
▦	Texture:	**Bold, soft**
☼	Light:	**Full sun to part shade**
📏	Size:	**2–4 ft. tall (6–8 ft. in flower), 2–3 ft. wide**

Character:

Medium to large evergreen succulent grown for bold texture, spiky rosette shape, white summer flower

Some good plants fall in with a tough crowd, and yucca is the leader of that pack. The original "parking lot plant," this native shows up too many unpretty places, so for all its virtues, it's usually seen as an unsavory character. Its flower towers do get attention, but its spikiness may be unwelcome.

RATTLESNAKE MASTER

Eryngium yuccifolium

Hardiness:
Zones 3–8

Shape:
Spiky rosette

Color:
Blue-green leaf, white flower

Texture:
Bold, soft

Light:
Full sun

Size:
2–3 ft. high and wide (4–5 ft. high in flower)

Character:

Medium herbaceous perennial grown for bold texture, spiky rosette shape, white summer flower

A Midwest-Southeast native, rattlesnake master makes a cool, blue-green rosette. In summer, it sends up tall antennae topped by fuzzy golf balls of bloom, favorites of beneficial insects. This low-water perennial's leaves vary in color a bit, so look for plants with lighter, bluer, more silvery leaves.

BLUE OAT GRASS

Helictotrichon sempervirens and cultivars

Hardiness:	Texture:
Zones 4–8	**Fine, soft**
Shape:	Light:
Spiky rosette	**Full sun**
Color:	Size:
Blue foliage	**2–3 ft. high and wide**

Character:
Medium herbaceous perennial grown for fine texture, blue multiseason foliage, spiky rosette shape

Though visually soft, the subtle architecture of this sky-blue grass can't be ignored—it's a pincushion of upright blades that give way to a gracefully bowed outer skirt. Blue oat grass blooms early summer in a veil of similarly subtle, ethereal flowers. It appreciates sun, drier soils, and low humidity.

275

YUCCA

DESERT SPOON

Dasylirion wheeleri

Hardiness:	Texture:
Zones 7–10	**Fine, soft**

Shape:	Light:
Spiky rosette	**Full sun**

Color:	Size:
Blue-gray-green foliage	**6–10 ft. high and wide**

Character:
Large evergreen succulent grown for fine texture, spiky rosette shape, year-round foliage in various colors

Like a giant electrified grass, desert spoon's wild and woolly explosion of foliage somehow makes an incredibly elegant statement in mild-climate gardens in spite of itself. This denizen of the Southwest and Mexico thrives in heat, drought, and poor soils, and many plants boast bright blue foliage to boot.

● ● ● ● ● ● ● ● ● ● ● ● ● ● ● ● ● ●

277

'Karley Rose' fountain grass (*Pennisetum orientale* 'Karley Rose') puts to rest the idea that all grasses are created brown.

Grasses and Groundcovers

One plant group that especially stands out from the garden crowd is grasses and ground covers. As special as they are, both tend to suffer identity crisis. Various grasses and groundcovers share qualities of shrubs, vines, and perennials, and like those other groups have their problems—some grasses and groundcovers are more likely to grow into thugs in their quest to be the best. That said, the all-star grasses and groundcovers that own their role shine especially brightly.

BAMBOO

Phyllostachys species

🌡	Hardiness:	**Zones 6–10**
☁	Shape:	**Upright, creeping**
⚒	Color:	**Yellow-green leaf and cane**
✹	Texture:	**Fine, glossy**
☼	Light:	**Full sun to part shade**
📏	Size:	**7–30 ft. or more high, indefinite spread**

Character:
Large evergreen grass grown for fine texture, upright shape, yellow-green year-round foliage

The largest of the true grasses, bamboos either run or clump, and the runners are the bullies that give bamboo a bad name. Some *Phyllostachys* species are invasive in much of the Southeast, and though all runners aren't invaders, they all need their space. Bamboos also don't do extreme drought.

GIANT MISCANTHUS

Miscanthus×giganteus

Hardiness:
Zones 4–10

Shape:
Upright, clumping

Color:
Pink flower, yellow-green cane

Texture:
Medium to fine, glossy

Light:
Full sun to light shade

Size:
8–12 ft. high, 4–5 ft. wide

Character:
Large herbaceous grass grown for fine texture, size, upright shape, pink fall flower

Giant miscanthus sends up a green pillar of vertical canes that burst into a bundle of leaves at the top. It blooms pink very late in summer, and unlike its miscanthus cousins, it's a sterile hybrid that stays put. This gentle giant is a snap in sun and average soil.

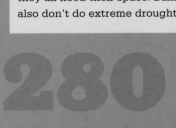

JAPANESE FOREST GRASS

Hakonechloa macra cultivars

Hardiness: **Zones 5–9**	Texture: **Fine, glossy**
Shape: **Prostrate, clumping**	Light: **Part shade to full shade**
Color: **Green, gold, or variegated leaf, red fall leaf in cultivars**	Size: **1–3 ft. high and wide**

Character:
**Small herbaceous grass grown for
fine texture, clumping shape, multiseason foliage in various colors**

Japanese forest grass brings a shimmering
mini bamboo grove to even the smallest of
gardens. This well-heeled plant is spellbinding
in shade, moderately dry shade included.
Gold-striped 'Aureola' sparkles, as does white-
striped 'Fubuki'. 'Beni-Kaze' is a green that
turns a spectacular red in fall.

BAMBOO

OCOTILLO

Fouquieria splendens

Hardiness:	Texture:
Zones 8–10	**Fine, glossy**
Shape:	Light:
Upright, clumping	**Full sun**
Color:	Size:
Orange flower, green stem	**15–20 ft. high, 8–10 ft. wide**

Character:
Large deciduous shrub grown for fine texture, upright shape, orange spring flower

Canes of giant ocotillo accentuate the desert landscape like bundles of exclamation points, topped with red-orange flowers after rains. Ocotillo needs good drainage—raised beds are best in all but true desert climates—and it loses its leaves in the dry season. Flowers attract birds and pollinators of all kinds.

BISHOP'S WEED

Aegopodium podagraria and cultivars

	Hardiness:	**Zones 4–9**
	Shape:	**Mounded, creeping**
	Color:	**Green or white-variegated leaf, white flower**
	Texture:	**Medium in leaf, fine in flower**
	Light:	**Full sun to full shade**
	Size:	**6–24 in. high, indefinite spread**

Character:
Small herbaceous groundcover grown for multiseason variegated foliage, creeping shape

A bully at its worst, variegated bishop's weed came to popularity as an easy spreading groundcover, especially for shade. It reverts to green and turns into a steamroller, smothering ecosystems in temperate regions across North America as an invasive species.

YELLOWROOT

Xanthorhiza simplicissima

Hardiness:
Zones 3–9

Shape:
Upright to mounded, creeping

Color:
Green leaf, red-purple fall leaf

Texture:
Medium to fine, glossy

Light:
Full sun to full shade

Size:
2–3 ft. high, 6 ft. or more wide

Character:
Medium deciduous groundcover grown for red-purple fall foliage, creeping shape

A native east of the Mississippi, yellowroot makes a tidy, shrubby groundcover for sun or shade, and its celery-like leaves turn a bold red-purple in fall. Yellowroot grows well in damp to moderately dry soils. Cut its oldest stems to the ground if they get too tall.

BISHOP'S WEED

CARPET BUGLE

Ajuga reptans and cultivars

Hardiness:
Zones 3–10

Shape:
Rosette to mounded, creeping

Color:
Red, green, purple, or white-variegated leaf, blue or white flower

Texture:
Medium in leaf, fine in flower, soft

Light:
Full sun to part shade

Size:
6–8 in. high, 12 in. or more wide

Character:
Small semievergreen groundcover grown for multiseason foliage in various colors, creeping shape

Easy and colorful, carpet bugle is a party girl with a bawdy palette of purples, reds, and whites, and blue or white flowers to boot. This outgoing groundcover spreads around merrily, but it's never out of hand. Adaptable bugle takes sun or shade, even moderately dry shade.

CREEPING RASPBERRY

Rubus pentalobus and cultivars

Hardiness:
Zones 6–9

Shape:
Prostrate, creeping

Color:
Green leaf, red-purple fall leaf

Texture:
Medium, soft

Light:
Full sun to part shade

Size:
4–6 in. high, indefinite spread

Character:
Small evergreen to herbaceous groundcover grown for soft texture, creeping shape

Creeping raspberry makes a cascading mat of crushed-velvet leaves, even on tough sites, and turns a bronzy fall red that lasts through winter in mild zones where it's evergreen. This groundcover makes a great spreader, but it's not a problem to keep in bounds.

• • • • • • • • • • • • • • • • • •

CREEPING JUNIPER

Juniperus horizontalis and cultivars

	Hardiness:	**Zones 3–9**
	Shape:	**Prostrate, creeping**
	Color:	**Green, gold, or blue leaf**
	Texture:	**Fine, soft**
	Light:	**Full sun**
	Size:	**6–12 in. high, 5–6 ft. wide**

Character:
Medium evergreen groundcover grown for year-round foliage, foliage in various colors in cultivars, creeping shape, fine texture

Another example of guilt by parking lot, creeping juniper grows great in difficult sites with heat and drought, but with the wrong crowd. So many gardeners prefer plants that don't grow at gas stations, and that is its downfall. Juniper also can't handle shade.

HEATHS AND HEATHERS

Erica and *Calluna* species and cultivars

Hardiness: **Zones 4–7**	Texture: **Fine, soft**
Shape: **Prostrate, creeping**	Light: **Full sun**
Color: **Pink, purple, or white flower, green or gold leaf**	Size: **1–2 ft. high and wide**

Character:
**Small evergreen groundcover grown
for spring or summer flower in
various colors, year-round foliage,
creeping shape, fine texture, gold
foliage in cultivars**

For rocky, sandy soils on the acidic side, heathers and heaths can't be beat. These tough, tidy characters grow tiny, needle-like leaves and equally tiny flowers—heaths (*Erica*, pictured) in earliest spring, and heathers (*Calluna*) in summer. Cultivars with colorful foliage are available too.

CREEPING JUNIPER

PROSTRATE JAPANESE PLUM YEW

Cephalotaxus harringtonia 'Prostrata'

Hardiness:
Zones (5)6–9

Shape:
Prostrate, spreading

Color:
Green leaf

Texture:
Fine, glossy

Light:
Part shade to full shade

Size:
2–3 ft. high, 3–6 ft. wide

Character:
Medium evergreen groundcover grown for year-round foliage, spreading shape, fine texture

This low-growing plum yew makes an ideal spreading groundcover, even for deep shade, its new growth reminiscent of a forest of tiny palms. It's actually a yew lookalike and takes dry shade once established. Unlike conventional yew, plum yew thrives in hot, humid climates, as well as cold.

CREEPING ROSEMARY

Rosmarinus officinalis 'Prostratus'

Hardiness: **Zones 8–10**	Texture: **Fine, soft**
Shape: **Prostrate, spreading**	Light: **Full sun to light shade**
Color: **Blue flower, green leaf**	Size: **6–12 in. high, 4–8 ft. wide**

Character:
Small evergreen groundcover grown for fragrant, edible year-round foliage, spreading shape, fine texture, blue summer flower

Since its parent plant is a Mediterranean native, this creeping rosemary knows heat and drought more than most. Like its parent, 'Prostrata' brings both intensely fragrant foliage and sky blue summer flowers to the garden.

● ● ● ● ● ● ● ● ● ● ● ● ● ● ●

DWARF FOUNTAIN GRASS

Pennisetum alopecuroides 'Hameln'

	Hardiness:	**Zones 5–9**
	Shape:	**Rounded, clumping**
	Color:	**White to tan flower, green leaf**
	Texture:	**Fine, soft**
	Light:	**Full sun**
	Size:	**1–3 ft. high and wide**

Character:

Medium herbaceous grass grown for white to tan fall flower, fine texture, rounded shape

Ornamental grasses took a while to catch on, and plain Jane 'Hameln' speaks to why: one of the earliest to become popular, it rarely stands out and fits the mouse-brown profile nongrass fans decry. Many and varied exciting other grasses are available today. Fountain grass also can't take shade.

HAIR GRASS

Deschampsia cespitosa / Deschampsia flexuosa

Hardiness:	Texture:
Zones 4–9	**Fine, soft**

Shape:	Light:
Rounded, clumping	**Full sun to part shade**

Color:	Size:
Chartreuse to white flower, green leaf	**1–3 ft. high, 1–2 ft. wide**

Character:
Medium herbaceous grass grown for chartreuse to white summer flower, fine texture, rounded shape

Tufted hair grass (*Deschampsia cespitosa*) and smaller crinkled hair grass (*D. flexuosa*) are native to temperate climates worldwide. Both thrive even in part shade (crinkled in dry shade) and send up smokestacks of pale apple-green flowers in summer. These bleach to white, a striking contrast against green foliage, and last into fall.

DWARF FOUNTAIN GRASS

ORIENTAL FOUNTAIN GRASS

Pennisetum orientale and cultivars

Hardiness:
Zones (5)6–8

Texture:
Fine, soft

Shape:
Rounded, clumping

Light:
Full sun to part sun

Color:
Pink or white flower, green leaf

Size:
3–4 ft. high and wide

Character:
Medium to large herbaceous grass grown for pink or white multiseason flower, fine texture, rounded shape

A long-blooming, low-water showstopper, oriental fountain grass gets the party started in early summer, and its seedheads stick around until fall, along with multiple bonus rounds of rebloom. Fabulous cultivar 'Karley Rose' (pictured) ups the ante with flowers in dusky pink.

MUHLY GRASS

Muhlenbergia capillaris and cultivars

Hardiness:
Zones 6–9

Shape:
Rounded, clumping

Color:
Pink or white flower, green leaf

Texture:
Fine, soft

Light:
Full sun

Size:
2–3 ft. high and wide

Character:
Medium herbaceous grass grown for pink or white fall flower, fine texture, rounded shape

For great color late in a grass or any plant, muhly is an all-star that can't be beat. This low-water western native explodes in puffy pink clouds of bloom late in the season and thrives in tough sites. Give muhly well-drained soil, especially where winters are wet, and it proves surprisingly hardy.

LAWN GRASS

Poa pratensis

🌡 Hardiness: **Zones 3–7**

🌳 Shape: **Mounded, creeping**

🎨 Color: **Green leaf**

Texture: **Fine, soft**

☀ Light: **Full sun to light shade**

📏 Size: **3–6 in. high and wide**

Character:
Small evergreen groundcover grown for creeping shape, fine texture, multiseason foliage

If there's a problem child that throws more tantrums than any other, it's lawn. This species, also called Kentucky bluegrass, is a popular lawn grass. Despite its name, it comes from Eurasia. As many a lawn enthusiast may find, it usually needs unsustainable levels of water, fertilizer, and maintenance. It also dislikes excess shade.

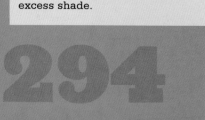

BUFFALO GRASS

Buchloe dactyloides

Hardiness:
Zones 3–9

Shape:
Mounded, creeping

Color:
Green leaf

Texture:
Fine, soft

Light:
Full sun

Size:
3–6 in. high and wide

Character:
Small evergreen groundcover grown for creeping shape, fine texture, multiseason foliage

A short grass gaining in popularity as all-star sustainable lawn is buffalo grass. This Great Plains native looks much like typical lawn, but it thrives in sun, heat, and drought, prefers to grow a bit taller, and requires less mowing. Outside buffalo's native range, cultivar 'Legacy' works better in the wetter East.

SEDGE

Carex pensylvanica / Carex appalachica

Hardiness:
Zones 3–7

Shape:
Vase, clumping

Color:
Green leaf

Texture:
Fine, soft

Light:
Part sun to part shade

Size:
6–12 in. high and wide

Character:
Small semievergreen groundcover or perennial grown for fine texture, multiseason foliage

Though they may be nearly identical to grasses, sedges belong to a group apart, and many make stupendous lawn for shady spots, even moderately dry shade. Two native species that are very lawnish are Appalachian sedge (*Carex appalachica*) and Pennsylvania sedge (*C. pensylvanica*, pictured).

LAWN GRASS

THYME

Thymus species

Hardiness:
Zones 4–9

Shape:
Prostrate, creeping

Color:
Green or silver leaf, red, pink, or white flower

Texture:
Medium to fine

Light:
Full sun to light shade

Size:
1–3 in. high, indefinite spread

Character:
Small evergreen or herbaceous groundcover grown for fragrant multiseason foliage, creeping shape, fine texture, multiseason flower in various colors

Thymes not only shine as herbs for cooking, they make deliciously fragrant, walkable groundcovers for hot, dry, or rocky sites. Standouts include tiny coconut thyme (*Thymus pulegioides* 'Coccineus', actually lemon-scented) and tinier creeping thyme (*Thymus serpyllum*). Give thyme sun and good drainage.

LILY OF THE VALLEY

Convallaria majalis

🌡	Hardiness:	**Zones 3–8**
☁	Shape:	**Upright, creeping**
🖌	Color:	**White flower, green leaf**
#	Texture:	**Medium in leaf, fine in flower**
☼	Light:	**Part shade to full shade**
📏	Size:	**6–12 in. high, indefinite spread**

Character:
Small herbaceous groundcover grown for fragrant white spring flower, upright shape

Fickle lily of the valley is the problem child that can't make up its mind. Plant it in damp soil, and a lily army will arise and wage war through the garden. If it's too dry, it wilts by midsummer. Beloved for sweet-scented spring flowers, its foliage is neat at its best, each plant lined up like a toy soldier.

SOLOMON'S SEAL

Polygonatum species and cultivars

Hardiness:
Zones 3–8

Shape:
Upright to arching, clumping

Color:
White flower, green or white-variegated leaf in cultivars

Texture:
Medium, glossy

Light:
Part shade to full shade

Size:
1–3 ft. high and wide

Character:
Small to medium herbaceous groundcover grown for arching shape, fragrant white spring flower, multiseason variegated foliage in cultivars

A boon to shade gardens of all kinds, Solomon's seal unfurls as the king of spring drama, follows up with scented bells of bloom and stately leaves throughout the growing season. It takes dry shade once established. 'Variegatum' has the added allure of white-edged foliage.

LILY OF THE VALLEY

CAST IRON PLANT

Aspidistra elatior and cultivars

Hardiness:
Zones (7)8–10

Shape:
Upright, clumping

Color:
Green or white-variegated leaf

Texture:
Bold, glossy

Light:
Part shade to full shade

Size:
2–3 ft. high and wide

Character:
Medium evergreen groundcover grown for bold texture, year-round foliage, upright shape

Cast iron plant is a bulletproof butterfly for shade or morning sun, its rafts of big leaves a billowy excess all year for difficult sites. Many showy variegated cultivars are available. If it gets tattered in winter in its northern range, remove damaged leaves for a new flush in spring.

'POORINDA ROYAL MANTLE' GREVILLEA

Grevillea 'Poorinda Royal Mantle'

Hardiness:
Zones 8b–10

Light:
**Full sun
to part shade**

Shape:
**Prostrate,
creeping**

Size:
**8–12 in. high,
indefinite spread**

Color:
**Red flower,
green leaf**

Texture:
**Medium in leaf,
fine in flower,
glossy**

Character:
**Small evergreen groundcover grown
for red summer flower, creeping
shape, fine texture**

For mild-climate gardeners with heat, drought, sun, or poor soil, this running grevillea is the all-star groundcover everyone will ask about. Its red toothbrush flowers are like fish swimming in a stream of shimmering, willowy leaves. Pollinators abound when 'Royal Mantle' blooms. It's hardier with well-drained soil.

● ● ● ● ● ● ● ● ● ● ● ● ● ●

MISCANTHUS

Miscanthus sinensis

	Hardiness:	**Zones (4)5–9**
	Shape:	**Upright, clumping**
	Color:	**Pink or white flower, white- or gold-variegated leaf in cultivars**
	Texture:	**Medium to fine**
	Light:	**Full sun to light shade**
	Size:	**4–6 ft. high, 2–4 ft. wide**

Character:
Large herbaceous grass grown for pink or white flower, fine texture, upright shape, variegated foliage in cultivars

It would seem to be the PTA mom to many popular cultivars, but Mother Miscanthus's invasiveness in the Mid-Atlantic has become a serious concern in recent years. While cultivars of this grass may not make viable seed, many gardeners prefer to play it safe and avoid early bloomers that could. Miscanthus's cold hardiness also varies.

FROST GRASS

Spodiopogon sibiricus

Hardiness:
Zones 5–9

Shape:
Upright, clumping

Color:
White flower, red fall leaf

Texture:
Medium to fine, glossy

Light:
Full sun

Size:
3–5 ft. high, 2–3 ft. wide

Character:
Large herbaceous grass grown for fine texture, upright shape, red fall foliage, white summer flower

For cold-climate gardeners in search of colorful, multiseason grasses, frost grass answers the call. This neat grass grows in a tight clump and sends up wiry, light-catching antennae of flower in late summer, but the real show comes in fall: if planted in sun, it puts on a spectacular show with fire-engine red foliage.

'NORTHWIND' SWITCH GRASS

Panicum virgatum 'Northwind'

Hardiness:
Zones 5–9

Shape:
Upright, clumping

Color:
White flower,
blue-green leaf

Texture:
Medium to
fine, soft

Light:
Full sun to
part shade

Size:
4–6 ft. high,
2–3 ft. wide

Character:
Large herbaceous grass grown for
white summer flower, fine texture,
upright shape, blue multiseason
foliage

Of many available switch grass cultivars, 'Northwind' makes an A+. A vertical sheath of blue-fading-to-green foliage, it bursts into a contrasting constellation of bloom in summer, and in fall fades to a buff color that lasts all winter. Easy-growing switch grasses take cold and heat, damp and drought.

MISCAN-THUS

'KARL FOERSTER' FEATHER REED GRASS

Calamagrostis acutiflora 'Karl Foerster'

Hardiness:
Zones 5–9

Shape:
Upright, clumping

Color:
Pink to tan flower, green leaf

Texture:
Fine, soft

Light:
Full sun to part shade

Size:
4–6 ft. high, 2–3 ft. wide

Character:
Large herbaceous grass grown for pink to tan multiseason flower; fine texture, upright shape

The classic beauty of ornamental grasses, well-known 'Karl Foerster' is a grass with staying power. Its neat column of green bursts into flurries of calico pink flower earlier than most grasses. These plumes turn to fawn in fall. 'Karl Foerster' shines in a range of climates and conditions, even clay soils.

• •

MOSS

Various species

🌡	Hardiness:	**Varies**
🍃	Shape:	**Mounded, creeping**
🖌	Color:	**Green leaf**
#	Texture:	**Fine, soft**
☼	Light:	**Full sun to full shade**
📏	Size:	**1–2 in. high, indefinite spread**

Character:

Small evergreen groundcover grown for year-round foliage, fine texture, creeping shape

Lots of different mosses grow naturally in lots of different places. Sometimes this shy, fuzzy plant is beloved by gardeners, but sometimes not. Moisture and color are the common thread between most mosses—most are mostly green, and most won't stand for drought.

CREEPING SEDUM

Sedum cultivars

Hardiness:
Zones 3–9

Shape:
Mounded, creeping

Color:
Red, yellow, green, blue, or purple leaf, pink, yellow, or white flower

Texture:
Fine to medium

Light:
Full sun to part shade

Size:
1–3 in. high, indefinite spread

Character:

Small evergreen or herbaceous groundcover grown for multiseason foliage in various colors, multiseason flower in various colors, fine texture, creeping shape

Creeping sedums make up one of the most versatile, varied, valuable groups in gardening. These little succulents thrive in blistering heat and drought, as well as average sites, and come in a crayon box of colors. Creeping sedums are happiest in well-drained soil, with sun or light shade.

MOSS

'PLATT'S BLACK' BRASS BUTTONS

Leptinella squalida 'Platt's Black'

Hardiness:
Zones 5–9

Shape:
Mounded, creeping

Color:
Black-purple to green leaf

Texture:
Fine, soft

Light:
Full sun to part shade

Size:
1–2 in. high, indefinite spread

Character:
Small evergreen or herbaceous groundcover grown for black-purple multiseason foliage, fine texture, creeping shape

Some people are always in search of something different. For those folks, 'Platt's Black' brass buttons brings a psychedelic black velvet canvas of groundcover to the garden. This plant likes average to damp soils, but takes brief dry spells with light shade or afternoon shade. It's sometimes sold as *Cotula squalida* 'Platt's Black'.

ICE PLANT

Delosperma species and cultivars

Hardiness:
Zones 4–9

Shape:
Mounded, creeping

Color:
Pink, yellow, purple, or white flower, green leaf

Texture:
Fine

Light:
Full sun

Size:
1–2 in. high, indefinite spread

Character:
Small herbaceous groundcover grown for multiseason flower in various colors, fine texture, creeping shape

Another succulent star, ice plant excels in hot, dry, rocky sites in mild climates, and this little plant blooms with eye-popping daisies on and off all season. Ice plant needs good drainage to survive, especially where winters tend to be wet. 'Kelaidis' is an especially excellent cultivar, pretty in pale pink, while 'Fire Spinner' is a wild orange and purple.

• • • • • • • • • • • • • • • • • •

PACHYSANDRA

Pachysandra terminalis

	Hardiness:	**Zones 5–9**
	Shape:	**Mounded, creeping**
	Color:	**Green leaf**
	Texture:	**Medium, glossy**
	Light:	**Part shade to full shade**
	Size:	**6–8 in. high, indefinite spread**

Character:
Small evergreen groundcover grown for year-round green leaf, creeping shape

If there were a trophy for boring groundcovers for shade, you'd be hard pressed to come up with a plant more qualified than pachysandra. This poor plant excels in the throes of difficult dry shade, but plain green pachysandra may forever be overplayed.

EUROPEAN GINGER

Asarum europaeum

Hardiness: **Zones 4–8**	Texture: **Bold, glossy**
Shape: **Mounded, creeping**	Light: **Part shade to full shade**
Color: **Green or white-variegated leaf**	Size: **4–6 in. high, 6–12 in. wide**

Character:
Small evergreen groundcover grown for bold texture, year-round green foliage, variegated foliage in cultivars

Reflective surfaces give shimmer to shady places, and no star shines brighter than a clump of European ginger. This seemingly succulent evergreen forms mats of heart-shaped leaves, each like a glinting makeup mirror, and thrives in average soils and even dry shade once established.

CREEPING MAHONIA

Mahonia repens

Hardiness:
Zones 5–8

Shape:
Upright, creeping

Color:
Green leaf, red winter leaf, yellow flower, purple fruit

Texture:
Medium, glossy

Light:
Full sun to part shade

Size:
6–12 in. high and wide

Character:
Small evergreen groundcover grown for year-round foliage, yellow spring flower, purple fall fruit, red winter foliage

An all-season native of the West, creeping mahonia bears dark, holly-like leaves, blooms in a smiley-face yellow in spring, follows that with purple berries, and ends with red-purple evergreen foliage for winter. Birds and pollinators enjoy its flower and fruit.

PACHY-SANDRA

ALLEGHENY PACHYSANDRA

Pachysandra procumbens

Hardiness:
Zones 4b–9

Shape:
Mounded, creeping

Color:
Green leaf

Texture:
Medium, soft

Light:
Part shade to full shade

Size:
6–12 in. high and wide

Character:
Small semievergreen groundcover grown for multiseason foliage, creeping shape

As its name suggests, Allegheny pachysandra is the American counterpart to its Japanese cousin. This semievergreen Southeast native makes for a patchwork carpet of soft greens in shade and grows at a more refined pace than its relative.

PAMPAS GRASS

Cortaderia selloana

🌡	Hardiness:	**Zones 8–10**
🌲	Shape:	**Rounded, clumping**
🔧	Color:	**White flower, green leaf**
⌗	Texture:	**Fine, soft**
☀	Light:	**Full sun**
📏	Size:	**6–12 ft. high, 4–6 ft. wide**

Character:
Large evergreen grass grown for white fall flower, fine texture, rounded shape

Giant pampas grass may seem respectable, with its rockets of bearded plumes in late summer, but this grass could be the big kid who steals your lunch. It's earned invasive species status in California, Texas, and other states in the West and Southeast. Pampas is also tender north of Zone 8.

INDIAN GRASS

Sorghastrum nutans and cultivars

Hardiness:
Zones 4–9

Shape:
Upright, clumping

Color:
White flower, blue-green leaf

Texture:
Fine, soft

Light:
Full sun

Size:
3–5 ft. high, 1–2 ft. wide

Character:
Medium to large herbaceous grass grown for white fall flower, multiseason blue-green foliage, fine texture, upright shape

A prairie native of all but westernmost North America, superhardy Indian grass grows straight as an arrow into a narrow, 3-foot clump of blue-green leaves—then sends up feathery plumes of bloom twice as high, a sight to see in late summer. Cultivars 'Sioux Blue' and 'Indian Steel' boast especially blue foliage.

PAMPAS GRASS

RAVENNA GRASS

Saccharum ravennae

Hardiness:
Zones 5–9

Shape:
Rounded, clumping

Color:
Pink to white flower; green leaf

Texture:
Fine, soft

Light:
Full sun

Size:
6–12 ft. high, 4–6 ft. wide

Character:
Large herbaceous grass grown for pink fall flower, fine texture, rounded shape

For cold-climate gardens where it won't get weedy, ravenna grass blooms with pink plumes as far north as Zone 5. This striking grass is similar but hardier and more colorful than pampas grass. It's shorter too, making it a bit more manageable, but flowers at twice the height—a whopping 12 feet.

CAPE RUSH

Chondropetalum tectorum

Hardiness:
Zones 9–10

Shape:
Rounded, clumping

Color:
Green leaf, brown flower

Texture:
Fine, soft

Light:
Full sun

Size:
4–6 ft. high and wide

Character:
Large evergreen grass grown for fine texture, rounded shape, brown summer flower

Few plants are as entrancing as a huge clump of cape rush. Each blade of this big grass seems to pulsate with wind and light, an optical illusion in plant form. In mild-climate gardens where it's hardy, cape rush thrives in wet sites or dry once established. More importantly, it's a noninvasive plant that stays put.

●●●●●●●●●●●●●●●●●●●

VINCA

Vinca minor

🌡	Hardiness:	**Zones 4–8**
🌲	Shape:	**Prostrate, creeping**
🔌	Color:	**Blue flower, green leaf**
▦	Texture:	**Fine, glossy**
☼	Light:	**Full sun to part shade**
📏	Size:	**3–6 in. high, indefinite spread**

Character:

Small evergreen groundcover grown for year-round foliage, creeping shape, fine texture, blue spring flower

An old-fashioned troublemaker with a taste for forest floors, vinca escapes cultivation and blankets native ecosystems in various regions all over the country. If that weren't enough, it's something of a snooze after it blooms with blue flowers in spring.

'GRO-LOW' SUMAC

Rhus aromatica 'Gro-Low'

Hardiness:
Zones 3–9

Shape:
Upright, creeping

Color:
Yellow flower, green leaf, red-orange fall leaf

Texture:
Fine, glossy

Light:
Full sun to part shade

Size:
1–2 ft. high, indefinite spread

Character:
Small deciduous groundcover grown for creeping shape, red-orange fall foliage, fine texture, yellow spring flower

A bubbling cauldron of groundcover, 'Gro-Low' is a cultivar of native aromatic sumac. This plant starts the year with little candles of pale yellow flowers, followed by glossy foliage that turns a blazing red in fall. Female plants fruit as well. 'Gro-Low' shines in sun or part shade in even the poorest soils.

'ROSE CARPET' INDIGO

Indigofera 'Rose Carpet'

Hardiness: **Zones 5–8**	Texture: **Fine, soft**
Shape: **Prostrate, creeping**	Light: **Full sun**
Color: **Pink flower, green leaf**	Size: **6–12 in. high, 12–48 in. wide**

Character:
Small deciduous groundcover grown for pink summer flower, creeping shape, fine texture

True to its name, 'Rose Carpet' indigo blooms pretty in summer pink with spikes of pea flowers, but that's not all: this delicate beauty's dense habit blocks weeds with aplomb, and it thrives even in lean, dry soil.

VINCA

GREEN AND GOLD

Chrysogonum virginianum

Hardiness:
Zones 5–9

Shape:
Mounded, creeping

Color:
Yellow flower, green leaf

Texture:
Fine to medium, glossy

Light:
Part shade to full shade

Size:
6–12 in. high, 6–18 in. wide

Character:
Small herbaceous groundcover or perennial grown for yellow multiseason flower, creeping shape

Green and gold makes a cheerful color guard for shade, its yellow daisies brightening most any dark corner. This Southeast native blooms on and off throughout the growing season. It spreads politely and grows well in average to damp garden conditions.

WINTERCREEPER

Euonymus fortunei and cultivars

🌡 Hardiness: **Zones 4–9**

🍃 Shape: **Prostrate, creeping or clinging**

🖌 Color: **Green, white- or gold-variegated leaf**

Texture: **Fine, glossy**

☀ Light: **Full sun to part shade**

📏 Size: **1–3 in. high, indefinite spread**

Character:
Small evergreen groundcover or vine grown for year-round foliage, variegated in cultivars, creeping or clinging shape, fine texture

Innocent little wintercreeper makes a pretty, tiny-leaved evergreen groundcover—or occasionally a climber—but it's a juvenile delinquent that quickly busts out of its garden boundaries. Wintercreeper invades natural areas in temperate regions of the United States.

BEARBERRY

Arctostaphylos uva-ursi and cultivars

Hardiness:
Zones 2–6

Shape:
Prostrate, creeping

Color:
Green leaf, red fruit

Texture:
Fine, glossy

Light:
Full sun to part shade

Size:
6–12 in. high, 36–48 in. wide

Character:
Small evergreen groundcover grown for year-round foliage, creeping shape, fine texture

A native of northern temperate zones worldwide, bearberry's neat, shiny, itsy bitsy leaves make it a popular evergreen groundcover among gardeners in the know. It grows especially well in hot, dry sites with poor soil, and its red berries in fall are a sure thing for bird love.

315

WINTER-CREEPER

LOWBUSH BLUEBERRY

Vaccinium angustifolium and cultivars

Hardiness: **Zones 3–7**	Texture: **Fine, glossy**
Shape: **Mounded, creeping**	Light: **Full sun to part shade**
Color: **Green leaf, red fall leaf**	Size: **6–24 in. high and wide**

Character:
Small deciduous groundcover grown for creeping shape, blue summer fruit, red fall foliage

Another northern native, lowbush blueberry is the little brother of its food-producing kin. This teeny berry boasts fiery red fall foliage, as well as miniature fruit adored by all manner of wildlife. (You can eat it too.) Lowbush adapts well to moist or moderately dry (even rocky) sites with acidic soil.

DWARF BOSTON IVY

Parthenocissus tricuspidata 'Lowii'

Hardiness:
Zones 3–9

Shape:
Prostrate, creeping or clinging

Color:
Green leaf, red fall leaf

Texture:
Fine, glossy

Light:
Full sun to part shade

Size:
30–50 ft. high, 5–10 ft. wide

Character:
Small deciduous groundcover or vine grown for clinging shape, fine texture, red fall foliage

For those in search of a wintercreeper alternative that climbs, dwarf Boston ivy wins hands down. Like its bigger parent, this petite plant turns a smoldering red in fall and grows easily up and over most any surface, albeit within its garden confines.

● ● ● ● ● ● ● ● ● ● ● ● ● ● ● ● ●

Resources

White fir (*Abies concolor*) and pink heath (*Erica*) make an all-star match.

Recommended Reading

Armitage, Allan M. 2006. *Armitage's Native Plants for North American Gardens.* Portland, Oregon: Timber Press.

Armitage, Allan M. 2011. *Armitage's Garden Perennials.* 2nd ed. Portland, Oregon: Timber Press.

Burrell, C. Colston. 2011. *Native Alternatives to Invasive Plants.* Brooklyn Botanic Garden Guides for a Greener Planet. Brooklyn, New York: Brooklyn Botanic Garden.

Darke, Rick. 2007. *The Encyclopedia of Grasses for Livable Landscapes.* Portland, Oregon: Timber Press.

Dirr, Michael A. 2011. *Dirr's Encyclopedia of Trees and Shrubs.* Portland, Oregon: Timber Press

DiSabato-Aust, Tracy. 2009. *50 High-Impact, Low-Care Garden Plants.* Portland, Oregon: Timber Press.

DiSabato-Aust, Tracy. 2006. *The Well-Tended Perennial Garden: Planting and Pruning Techniques.* Expanded ed. Portland, Oregon: Timber Press.

Odenwald, Neil G., and James R. Turner. 2010. *Identification, Selection, and Use of Southern Plants for Landscape Design.* 4th rev. ed. Baton Rouge, Louisiana: Claitor's Publishing Division.

Ogden, Lauren Springer, and Scott Ogden. 2008. *Plant-Driven Design: Creating Gardens That Honor Plants, Place, and Spirit.* Portland, Oregon: Timber Press.

Ogden, Lauren Springer, and Scott Ogden. 2011. *Waterwise Plants for Sustainable Gardens: 200 Drought-Tolerant Choices for All Climates.* Portland, Oregon: Timber Press.

Ondra, Nancy J. 2007. *Foliage: Astonishing Color and Texture Beyond Flowers.* North Adams, Massachusetts: Storey Publishing.

Oudolf, Piet, with Noel Kingsbury. 1999. *Designing with Plants.* Portland, Oregon: Timber Press.

Reich, Lee. 2009. *Landscaping with Fruit: A Homeowner's Guide.* North Adams, Massachusetts: Storey Publishing.

Taylor, Jane. 1993. *Drought-Tolerant Plants: Waterwise Gardening for Every Climate.* New York: Prentice Hall.

Web Sites with More Information

Dave's Garden PlantFiles
davesgarden.com/guides/pf

Fine Gardening Plant Guide
finegardening.com/plantguide

Floridata
floridata.com

Great Plant Picks
greatplantpicks.org

Lady Bird Johnson Wildflower Center Native Plant Database
wildflower.org/plants

Missouri Botanical Garden Kemper Center for Home Gardening Plant Finder
missouribotanicalgarden.org/
gardens-gardening/your-garden/
plant-finder.aspx

North Carolina State University College of Agriculture and Life Sciences Plant Fact Sheets
ces.ncsu.edu/depts/hort/
consumer/factsheets/index.html

Plant Information Online— University of Minnesota
plantinfo.umn.edu

Plant Lust
plantlust.com

Plant Select
plantselect.org

Santa Fe Botanical Garden Plant Database
santafebotanicalgarden.org/
explore-nature/plant-database

Sunset Plant Finder
plantfinder.sunset.com

The Battery Plant Database
thebattery.org/plants

UC Davis Arboretum All-Stars
arboretum.ucdavis.edu/
arboretum_all_stars.aspx

University of Connecticut Plant Database
www.hort.uconn.edu/plants

University of Florida Institute of Food and Agricultural Sciences Southern Trees Fact Sheets
edis.ifas.ufl.edu/
department_envhort-trees

Mail-Order Sources for Plants

United States

Annie's Annuals
Richmond, California
(888) 266-4370
www.anniesannuals.com

Antique Rose Emporium
Brenham, Texas
(800) 441-0002
www.antiqueroseemporium.com

Arrowhead Alpines
Fowlerville, Michigan
(517) 223-3581
www.arrowhead-alpines.com

Avant Gardens
Dartmouth, Massachusetts
(508) 998-8819
www.avantgardensne.com

Big Dipper Farm
Black Diamond, Washington
(360) 886-8253
www.bigdipperfarm.com

Bluestone Perennials
Madison, Ohio
(800) 852-5243
www.bluestoneperennials.com

Brent and Becky's Bulbs
Gloucester, Virginia
(877) 661-2852
www.brentandbeckysbulbs.com

Broken Arrow Nursery
Hamden, Connecticut
(203) 288-1026
www.brokenarrownursery.com

Brushwood Nursery
Athens, Georgia
(706) 548-1710
www.gardenvines.com

Burnt Ridge Nursery
Onalaska, Washington
(360) 985-2873
www.burntridgenursery.com

Cistus Nursery
Portland, Oregon
(503) 621-2233
www.cistus.com

Dancing Oaks Nursery
Monmouth, Oregon
(503) 838-6058
www.dancingoaks.com

Digging Dog Nursery
Albion, California
(707) 937-1130
www.diggingdog.com

Dove Creek Gardens
Millington, Tennessee
(901) 829-2306
www.dovecreekgardens.com

Fairweather Gardens
Greenwich, New Jersey
(856) 451-6261
www.fairweathergardens.com

Fedco Trees
Waterville, Maine
(207) 873-7333
www.fedcoseeds.com/trees.htm

Forestfarm
Williams, Oregon
(541) 846-7269
www.forestfarm.com

Gardensoyvey.com
Arlington, Tennessee
(888) 617-7390
www.gardensoyvey.com

Gossler Farms
Springfield, Oregon
(541) 746-3922
www.gosslerfarms.com

Heronswood Nursery
Warminster, Pennsylvania
(877) 674-4714
www.heronswood.com

High Country Gardens
Santa Fe, New Mexico
(800) 925-9387
www.highcountrygardens.com

Joy Creek Nursery
Scappoose, Oregon
(503) 543-7474
www.joycreek.com

Klehm's Song Sparrow
Avalon, Wisconsin
(800) 553-3715
www.songsparrow.com

Lazy S'S Farm Nursery
Barboursville, Virginia
www.lazyssfarm.com

Mail-Order Natives
Lee, Florida
(850) 973-6830
www.mailordernatives.com

Nearly Native Nursery
Fayetteville, Georgia
(770) 460-6284
www.nearlynativenursery.com

Plant Delights Nursery
Raleigh, North Carolina
(919) 772-4794
www.plantdelights.com

Prairie Nursery
Westfield, Wisconsin
(800) 476-9453
www.prairienursery.com

RareFind Nursery
Jackson, New Jersey
(732) 833-0613
www.rarefindnursery.com

Sunshine Farm and Gardens
Renick, West Virginia
(304) 497-2208
www.sunfarm.com

United States
(continued)

Tripple Brook Farm
Southampton, Massachusetts
(413) 527-4626
www.tripplebrookfarm.com

Variegated Foliage Nursery
Eastford, Connecticut
(860) 974-3951
www.variegatedfoliage.com

White Flower Farm
Litchfield, Connecticut
(800) 503-9624
www.whiteflowerfarm.com

Woodlanders
Aiken, South Carolina
(803) 648-7522
www.woodlanders.net

Yucca Do Nursery
Giddings, Texas
(979) 542-8811
www.yuccado.com

Canada

Bluestem Nursery
Christina Lake, British Columbia
(250) 447-6363
www.bluestem.ca

Botanus
Langley, British Columbia
(800) 672-3413
www.botanus.com

Chuck Chapman Iris
Guelph, Ontario
(519) 856-0956
www.chapmaniris.com

Fraser's Thimble Farms
Salt Spring Island, British Columbia
(250) 537-5788
www.thimblefarms.com

Gardenimport
Richmond Hill, Ontario
(800) 339-8314
www.gardenimport.com

Hortico
Waterdown, Ontario
(905) 689-6984
www.hortico.com

Wildflower Farm
Coldwater, Ontario
(866) 476-9453
www.wildflowerfarm.com

Metric Conversions

inches to centimeters

inches	centimeters
1 in.	2.5 cm
2 in.	5 cm
3 in.	7.5 cm
4 in.	10 cm
5 in.	13 cm
6 in.	15 cm
7 in.	17 cm
8 in.	20 cm
9 in.	23 cm
10 in.	25 cm
12 in.	30 cm
15 in.	38 cm
18 in.	45 cm
24 in.	60 cm
30 in.	75 cm
36 in.	90 cm
48 in.	120 cm

feet to meters

feet	meters	feet	meters
1 ft.	0.3 m	25 ft.	7.5 m
2 ft.	0.6 m	30 ft.	9 m
3 ft.	0.9 m	35 ft.	10.5
4 ft.	1.2 m	40 ft.	12 m
5 ft.	1.5 m	50 ft.	15 m
6 ft.	1.8 m	60 ft.	19 m
7 ft.	2.1 m	70 ft.	21 m
8 ft.	2.4 m	80 ft.	24 m
9 ft.	2.7 m	90 ft.	27 m
10 ft.	3 m	100 ft.	30 m
15 ft.	5.4 m	200 ft.	60 m
20 ft.	6 m		

Photography Credits

All photos by Andrew Keys except as noted below:

arrowlakelass@Flickr: p. 53
Lynn Felici-Gallant: p. 157, left
Michelle Forman: p. 285
GAP Photos/Thomas Alamy: p. 200; p. 230
GAP Photos/Mark Bolton: p. 242
GAP Photos/Elke Borkowski: p. 278
GAP Photos/Christa Brand: p. 12
GAP Photos/Marg Cousens: p. 192
GAP Photos/Paul Debois: p. 259
GAP Photos/Marcus Harpur: p. 318
GAP Photos/Howard Rice: p. 197
GAP Photos/J. S. Sira: p. 100
Megan Hansen: p. 166
Annie Hayes: p. 184; p. 304; p. 305
Scott Hokunson: p. 140
Madge Holder: p. 190
Saxon Holt: p. 45
iStockphoto.com/AntiMartina: p. 180
iStockphoto.com/Barbara Cantiello: p. 163
iStockphoto.com/bb-foto: p. 65, left
iStockphoto.com/Blue Magic Photography: p. 264, left
iStockphoto.com/brytta: p. 150, left
iStockphoto.com/dexns: p. 194, left

iStockphoto.com/Earl Eliason: p. 246
iStockphoto.com/Rob Ellis: p. 39, left
iStockphoto.com/Eppic Photography: p. 32
iStockphoto.com/Jill Fromer: p. 282
iStockphoto.com/Steve Geer: p. 188, right
iStockphoto.com/Lijuan Guo: p. 18
iStockphoto.com/Steve Heck: p. 74
iStockphoto.com/hmlCA: p. 61
iStockphoto.com/Diane Labombarbe: p. 182, left
iStockphoto.com/Olga Lipatova: p. 254, right
iStockphoto.com/Pavlo Lutsan: p. 162
iStockphoto.com/Karen Massier: p. 257, right
iStockphoto.com/C. J. McKendry: p. 14
iStockphoto.com/James Metcalf: p. 269
iStockphoto.com/PuiYuen Ng: p. 179
iStockphoto.com/Greg Okimi: p. 155
iStockphoto.com/Stacey Putnam Photography: p. 34
iStockphoto.com/Lidia Rakcheeva: p. 135
iStockphoto.com/Dustin K. Ryan: p. 75, left
iStockphoto.com/Murphy Shewchuk: p. 258; p. 268
iStockphoto.com/Ron Thomas: p. 87, right
iStockphoto.com/zorani: p. 237
Brian Katzen: p. 336

Index

A

abelia, 154
Abelia ×grandiflora, 154
Abelia mosanensis, 154
Abies concolor, 46, 319
Abies firma, 47
Acacia baileyana 'Purpurea', 96
Acanthus mollis, 203
Acanthus spinosus, 203
acanthus, 203
Acanthus, 203
Acca sellowiana, 93
Acer circinatum, 33, 74
Acer griseum, 73
Acer macrophyllum, 89
Acer palmatum, 33, 72–74
Acer platanoides, 87–89
   'Crimson King', 87
Acer rubrum, 88
Acer saccharum, 87
Achillea, 232
   'Anthea', 232
   'Coronation Gold', 232
Aegopodium podagraria 'Variegatum',
   283–285
Agastache 'Blue Fortune', 225
agave, 202–204
Agave, 202–204
Ageratina altissima 'Chocolate', 208
Ajuga reptans, 284
Albizia julibrissin, 84–86
Allegheny pachysandra, 308
alstroemeria, 223
Alstroemeria, 223
   'Freedom', 223
   'Mauve Majesty', 223
   'Sweet Laura', 223
   'Tangerine Tango', 223
Ambrosia, 244

Amelanchier arborea, 94
Amelanchier ×grandiflora
   'Robin Hill', 94
Amelanchier laevis, 94
American bittersweet, 182
American sycamore, 43
American wisteria, 198
angel trumpet, 9
Apios americana, 197
Appalachian sedge, 295
Aralia elata, 147
   'Aureovariegata', 147
   'Silver Umbrellas', 147
   'Variegata', 100
Aralia spinosa, 147
aralia, 147
arborvitae, 102–104
Arbutus 'Marina', 51
Arctostaphylos uva-ursi, 315
Arizona cypress, 48
Aruncus aethusifolius, 206
Aruncus dioicus, 206
Asarum europaeum, 306
Asclepias speciosa, 215
Asclepias syriaca, 215
Asclepias tuberosa, 245
Asian bittersweet, 182–184
Asian plane, 43
Aspidistra elatior, 298
aster, 220
astilbe, 18, 205–207
Astilbe, 18, 205–207
Athyrium filix-femina, 231–233
aucuba, 137
Aucuba japonica, 137
Australian willow, 99

B

baby's breath, 208–210

'Baggesen's Gold' box honeysuckle, 106
baldcypresses, 66
'Ballerina' rose, 189
bamboo, 280–282
banana, 36–38
baptisia, 110
Baptisia, 110
barberry, 105–107
bay, 39–41
bayberry, 39
bearberry, 315
Berberis thunbergii, 105–107
Berberis vulgaris, 105–107
Bergenia, 271
Bergenia cordifolia, 271
Bergenia 'Lunar Glow', 250
Betula nigra, 98
   'Heritage', 98
Betula papyrifera, 42–45
bigleaf magnolia, 37
bigleaf maple, 89
Bignonia capreolata, 183
   'Tangerine Beauty', 183
bigroot geranium, 211
birch, 42–45
birchleaf, 155
bishop's weed, 283–285
blazing star, 241
bleeding heart, 211-213
'Blue Fortune' anise hyssop, 225
'Blue Mist' dwarf fothergilla, 158
blue oat grass, 275
'Blue Satin' rose of Sharon, 70
'Blue Shadow' fothergilla, 158
blue spruce, 46–48
bluebeard, 256
blueberry, 114
'Bluebird' mountain hydrangea, 140
blue-eyed Mary, 237
Boston ivy, 180, 191

bowman's root, 209
boxwood, 108–111
Brachysema praemosum 'Bronze Butterfly', 107
bridal wreath, 273
'Bronze Butterfly' shrub, 107
bronze birch borer, 42
Brugmansia, 9
brunnera, 248
Brunnera macrophylla, 248
    'Jack Frost', 248
    'King's Ransom', 248
    'Looking Glass', 248
Buchloe dactyloides, 294
    'Legacy', 294
Buddleia alternifolia, 159
    'Argentea', 159
Buddleia davidii, 145
buffalo grass, 294
bur oak, 75
burning bush, 112–115
bush clover, 172
butterfly bush, 145
butterfly ginger, 243
butterfly weed, 245
Buxus, 108–111

C

Caesalpinia pulcherimma, 86
Calamagrostis acutiflora 'Karl Foerster', 302
calamint, 210
Calamintha nepeta, 210
    'Blue Cloud', 210
    'White Cloud', 210
Calia secundiflora, 71
California honeysuckle, 196
California lilac, 146
callery pear, 49–51
Callirhoe involucrata, 264
Calluna, 287
Calocedrus decurrens, 67
Calycanthus floridus, 122
    'Athens', 122

camellia, 116–118
Camellia japonica, 116–118
Camellia sasanqua, 117
Campsis grandiflora 'Morning Calm', 182
canna, 214–217
Canna, 214–217
Cape rush, 311
Carex appalachica, 295
Carex muskingumensis, 233
    'Oehme', 233
Carex pensylvanica, 295
Carnegiea gigantea, 80
Carolina allspice, 122
Carolina lupine, 239
carpet bugle, 284
Carpinus betulus 'Fastigiata', 78
Caryopteris ×clandonensis, 256
    'Longwood Blue', 256
    'Worcester Gold', 256
cast iron plant, 298
catalpa, 36, 58
Catalpa 'Aurea', 36
Catalpa bignoniodes, 58
Catalpa 'Purpurea', 36
ceanothus, 175
Ceanothus ×pallidus 'Marie Bleu', 175
Ceanothus ×pallidus 'Marie Simon', 175
Ceanothus thyrsiflorus, 146
Ceiba speciosa, 61
celandine poppy, 265
Celastrus orbiculatus, 182–184
Celastrus scandens, 182
Cephalotaxus harringtonia, 178
    'Fastigiata', 178
    'Prostrata', 178, 288
Ceratostigma plumbaginoides, 236
Cercidiphyllum japonicum, 77
    'Morioka Weeping', 97
    'Pendula', 97
Cercis canadensis, 34, 69
    'Forest Pansy', 69
    'Hearts of Gold', 69
Cercocarpus, 155

Cercocarpus betuloides var. *blanchae*, 155
Cercocarpus ledifolius, 155
Chaenomeles speciosa 'Contorta', 132
character, in garden design, 22–23
Chilopsis linearis, 58
Chinese dogwood, 57
Chinese forest grass, 281
Chinese fringe tree, 95
Chinese indigo, 121
Chionanthus retusus, 95
×*Chitalpa tashkentensis* 'Morning Cloud', 58
'Chocolate' snakeroot, 208
Choisya 'Aztec Pearl', 166
Choisya ternata, 166
    'Sundance', 66
Chondropetalum tectorum, 311
chrysanthemum, 218–221
Chrysanthemum, 218–221
Chrysogonum virginianum, 314
Chrysothamnus nauseosus, 246
Cistus, 169
Cistus ×purpureus, 169
Cistus 'Sunset', 169
Citrus, 52–55
Citrus ×meyeri, 55
citrus trees, 52–55
Cladrastis kentukea, 85
    'Rosea', 85
clematis, large flowered, 185–187
Clematis, large-flowered, 185–187
Clematis integrifolia 'Rooguchi', 186
Clematis virginiana, 185
clematis wilt, 185
Clethra alnifolia, 123
    'Hummingbird', 123
    'Rosea', 123
    'Ruby Spice', 123
    'Sixteen Candles', 123
climbing rose, 188–190
coconut thyme, 296
color, in garden design, 20–21
Colorado blue spruce, 46

Comptonia peregrina, 231
cone cactus, 80
coneflower, 219
Confederate rose, 259
contorted flowering quince, 132
contorted hardy orange, 133
Convallaria majalis, 297–299
coral pea, 199
coralberry, 135
corkscrew willow, 131
Cornus alternifolia, 56
Cornus florida, 56–58
Cornus kousa, 57
Cortaderia selloana, 309–311
Corylopsis spicata, 128
   'Golden Spring', 128
Corylus avellana 'Contorta', 131–133
Crambe maritima, 202
crape myrtle, 119–121
creeping juniper, 286–289
creeping mahonia, 307
creeping raspberry, 285
creeping rosemary, 289
creeping sedum, 13, 303
creeping thyme, 296
crinkled hair grass, 291
crinum, 224
Crinum, 224
cross vine, 183
cucumber magnolia, 81
Cupressus arizonica, 48
   'Blue Ice', 48
   'Blue Pyramid', 48
Cupressus sempervirens, 65–67
cushion spurge, 221
cutleaf mountain mahogany, 155
Cylindropuntia imbricata, 269
Cytisus scoparius, 170–172

D

daphne, 122–124
Daphne, 122–124
dappled willow, 171
Dasylirion wheeleri, 277

dawn redwood, 63
daylily, 222–224
'Degroot's Spire' arborvitae, 65
delphinium, 225–227
Delphinium, 225–227
Delosperma, 305
   'Kelaidis', 305
Deschampsia cespitosa, 291
Deschampsia flexuosa, 291
desert spoon, 277
desert willow, 58
deutzia, 174
Deutzia gracilis, 174
   'Chardonnay Pearls', 23, 174
devil's walkingstick, 147
Dicentra spectabilis, 211–213
Dictamnus albus, 238
Dierama pulcherimmum, 213
Digitalis purpurea, 238–240
disease-resistant elm, 60
dogwood, 56–58
dogwood anthracnose, 56
drought, 25, 26, 28
dusty miller, 13, 228–230
Dutch elm disease, 59
dwarf Boston ivy, 317
dwarf fothergilla, 158
dwarf fountain grass, 290–293
dwarf goatsbeard, 206
dwarf Joe Pye weed, 260
dwarf palmetto, 9
dwarf rhododendron, 14, 125–127

E

Eastern prickly pear, 267
Eastern red cedar, 62, 142
Eastern wahoo, 113
Echinacea purpurea, 219
   'Hot Papaya', 219
   'Milkshake', 219
   'Southern Belle', 219
Echinopsis pachanoi, 80
Elaeagnus multiflora, 91
elderberry, 72

elecampane, 217
elm, 59–61
English ivy, 180, 191–193
enkianthus, 151
Enkianthus campanulatus, 151
   'Red Bells', 151
   'Showy Lantern', 151
Ensete, 36
Erica, 287, 319
Ericameria nauseosa, 246
Eriobotrya japonica, 38
Eryngium yuccifolium, 274
Eucommia ulmoides, 59
Euonymus alatus, 112–115
Euonymus atropurpureus, 113
Euonymus fortunei, 315–317
Eupatoriadelphus dubius 'Little Joe', 260
Eupatorium dubium 'Little Joe', 260
Eupatorium rugosum 'Chocolate', 208
Euphorbia polychroma, 221
   'Bonfire', 221
   'First Blush', 221
European beech, 76
European ginger, 306

F

Fagus sylvatica, 76
fairy wand, 213
Fallugia paradoxa, 118
false aloe, 204
fantail willow, 157
'Fastigiata' hornbeam, 78
Feijoa sellowiana, 93
fencepost cacti, 80
fern, 231–233
fertilizer, 9
Ficus benjamina, 136
fleece flower, 18, 200, 207
Florida star anise, 41
floss silk tree, 61
foamflower, 272
foothill penstemon, 226
Forestiera pubescens var. *neomexicana*,

45
forget-me-not, 234–237
forsythia, 128–130
Forsythia, 128–130
fothergilla, 158
Fothergilla gardenii, 158
   'Blue Mist', 158
Fothergilla ×intermedia 'Blue Shadow', 158
Fothergilla major, 158
fountain butterfly bush, 159
Fouquieria splendens, 282
foxglove, 238–240
fragrant abelia, 154
fragrant sumac, 115
Francoa sonchifolia, 273
   'Rogerson's Form', 273
frost grass, 300

G

garden maintenance, 27
gas plant, 238
Gastrolobium praemorsum 'Bronze Butterfly', 107
gaura, 212
Gaura lindheimeri, 212
Geijera parviflora, 99
geography, 27–28
Geranium macrorrhizum, 211
   'Bevan's Variety', 211
   'Ingwersen's Variety', 211
Geum triflorum, 205
giant fleece flower, 120
giant miscanthus, 280
Gillenia trifoliata, 209
gladiolus, 241–243
Gladiolus, 241–243
Gladiolus 'Boone', 242
Gladiolus 'Carolina Primrose', 242
Gladiolus communis subsp. *byzantinus*, 242
Gleditsia triacanthos var. *inermis*, 84
gloriosa lily, 184
Gloriosa superba, 184

glossy abelia, 154
goatsbeard, 206
golden lace, 247
goldenrod, 244–247
gold-leaved yew, 177
goumi, 91
grasses, 16, 279, 280, 290, 294
green and gold, 314
'Green Giant' arborvitae, 103
Grevillea 'Poorinda Royal Mantle', 299
Grevillea 'Robyn Gordon', 153
'Grey Owl' juniper, 142
'Gro-Low' sumac, 312
groundnut, 197
Gypsophila paniculata, 208–210

H

hair grass, 291
Hakonechloa macra, 281
   'Aureola', 281
   'Beni-Kaze', 281
   'Fubuki', 281
Hardenbergia violacea, 199
hardhack spirea, 173
hardiness, 23–25
hardy gladiolus, 242
hardy orange, 52
hardy rubber tree, 59
Harry Lauder's walking stick, 131–133
heath, 287, 319
heather, 287
Hedera helix, 180, 191–193
Hedychium, 243
Hedychium 'Doctor Moy', 243
Hedychium 'Tahitian Flame', 243
'Helene von Stein' lamb's ear, 229
Helictotrichon sempervirens, 275
hellebore, 257
Helleborus ×hybridus, 257
hellstrips, 141
Hemerocallis, 222–224
Hemerocallis 'Golden Zebra', 222
Hemerocallis 'Kwanso Variegata', 222
hemlock, 62–64

Heptacodium miconioides, 44
Hibiscus mutabilis, 259
Hibiscus syriacus 'Blue Satin', 70
highbush blueberry, 114
Hippophae rhamnoides, 162
holly, 134–137
honeylocust, 84
hosta, 248–250
Hosta, 248–250
Howell's Dwarf Tigertail' spruce, 143
hydrangea, 138–140
Hydrangea arborescens 'Invincibelle Spirit', 138
Hydrangea macrophylla, 138–140
Hydrangea serrata 'Bluebird', 140
Hylotelephium 'Matrona', 263
Hypericum frondosum 'Sunburst', 130
hyssop, 254
Hyssopus officinalis, 254

I

ice plant, 305
Ilex aquifolium, 134–137
Ilex glabra, 109
   'Compacta', 109
   'Densa', 109
   'Shamrock', 109
Ilex pedunculosa, 136
Ilex verticillata, 161
Ilex vomitoria, 104
Illicium, 41
Illicium anisatum, 41
Illicium floridanum, 41
Illicium henryi, 41
incense cedar, 67
Indian grass, 309
Indigofera amblyantha, 121
Indigofera 'Rose Carpet', 313
inkberry, 109
Inula magnifica, 217
'Invincibelle Spirit' smooth hydrangea, 138
iris, bearded, 251–253
iris, Louisiana iris types, 153

Iris pallida 'Argentea Variegata', 251
Iris pallida 'Variegata', 251
Iris tectorum, 252
ironweed, 261
Italian cypress, 65–67

J

jacaranda, 34, 68–71
Jacaranda, 68–71
Japanese arborvitae, 103
Japanese fir, 47
Japanese honeysuckle, 194–196
Japanese maple, 33, 72–74
Japanese roof iris, 252
Japanese spirea, 173
Japanese tree lilac, 119
Japanese umbrella pine, 64
Japanese yew, 179
juniper, 141–143
Juniperus horizontalis, 286–289
Juniperus ×*pfitzeriana*, 141–143
Juniperus scopulorum 'Skyrocket', 102
Juniperus scopulorum 'Wichita Blue', 102
Juniperus virginiana, 62, 142
  'Grey Owl', 142

K

Kalmia latifolia, 14, 125
'Karl Foerster' feather reed grass, 302
'Karley Rose' fountain grass, 278
katsura, 77
Kentucky bluegrass, 294
kerria, 170
Kerria japonica, 170
  'Golden Guinea', 170
  'Picta', 170
kohuhu, 156
'Kintzley's Ghost' grape honeysuckle, 194
Korean spice viburnum, 144
kudzu, 182

L

lady fern, 231
Lagerstroemia indica, 119–121
lamb's ear, 13
large fothergilla, 158
Laurus nobilis, 39–41
Lavandula, 254–256
lavender, 254–256
lawn grass, 294–296
lemon, 52
Leptinella squalida 'Platt's Black', 304
Lespedeza thunbergii, 172
Leucophyllum frutescens, 111, 127
  'Compacta', 127
Leucophyllum langmaniae, 111
  'Lynn's Legacy', 111
  'Rio Bravo', 111
leucothoe, 152
Leucothoe, 152
  'Rainbow', 152
  'Scarletta', 152
Lewis' mock orange, 53
Liatris, 241
Liatris pycnostachya, 241
Liatris spicata, 241
  'Alba, 241
  'Kobold', 241
light, 25
Ligustrum sinense, 154–146
Ligustrum vulgare, 154–156
lilac, 144–146
lily of the valley, 297–299
lime, 52
Liquidambar styraciflua 'Slender Silhouette', 79
'Little Gem' magnolia, 165
littleleaf linden, 49
live oak, 75–77
Lombardy poplar, 78–80
London plane, 43
longstalk holly, 136
Lonicera hispidula, 196
Lonicera japonica, 194–196

Lonicera nitida 'Baggesen's Gold', 106
Lonicera reticulata 'Kintzley's Ghost', 194
Lonicera sempervirens 'Major Wheeler', 195
loquat, 38
Louisiana iris, 253
lowbush blueberry, 316
low-care plants, 16, 50, 167, 168
'Lunar Glow' bergenia, 250

M

magnolia, 81–83
Magnolia acuminata, 81
  'Koban Dori', 81
Magnolia 'Butterflies', 81
Magnolia 'Elizabeth', 81
Magnolia grandiflora, 81–83
  'Little Gem', 165
Magnolia macrophylla, 37
Magnolia sieboldii, 83
  'Colossus', 83
Magnolia tripetala, 37
Magnolia virginiana, 82
Mahonia haematocarpa, 129
Mahonia repens, 307
'Major Wheeler' coral honeysuckle, 195
Malus cultivars, 94–96
Manfreda maculosa, 204
Manfreda 'Spot', 204
Manfreda virginica, 204
'Marina' strawberry tree, 51
'Matrona' sedum, 263
Metasequoia glyptostroboides, 63
Mexican orange, 166
Meyer lemon, 55
milkweed, 215
mimosa, 84–86
'Miniature Snowflake' mock orange, 167
miscanthus, 300–302
Miscanthus ×*giganteus*, 280
Miscanthus sinensis, 300–302
'Moonlight' climbing hydrangea, 193

'Morning Calm' Chinese trumpet creeper, 182
'Morning Cloud' chitalpa, 58
moss, 303–305
mountain laurel, 14, 125
mountain mahogany, 155
mountain mint, 228
mugo pine, 141
Muhlenbergia capillaris, 293
muhly grass, 293
mullein, 240
Musa, 36–38
Myosotis, 234–237
Myrica pensylvanica, 39

nannyberry, 139
native plants, 16
needle palm, 149
Neobuxbaumia polylopha, 80
Nepeta ×faassenii 'Walker's Low', 255
New Mexico privet, 45
ninebark, 105
'Northwind' switch grass, 301
Norway maple, 87–89
Nyssa sylvatica, 50

ocotillo, 282
Olea europaea, 90–93
olive, 90–93
Omphalodes cappadocica, 237
    'Starry Eyes', 237
Opuntia ellisiana, 258
Opuntia ficus-indica, 267–269
Opuntia humifusa, 258, 267
Opuntia polyacantha, 258, 268
orange, 52
Oriental fountain grass, 292
ornamental cherry tree, 94
ornamental crabapple tree, 94
ornamental fruit trees, 94–96
ornamental plum tree, 94
Osmanthus fragrans, 124

'Otto Luyken' English laurel, 40
Oyama magnolia, 83

P

Pachycereus marginatus, 80
pachysandra, 306–308
Pachysandra procumbens, 308
Pachysandra terminalis, 306–308
Paeonia lactiflora, 257–259
pagoda dogwood, 56
palm, 147–149
palm sedge, 233
pampas grass, 309–311
Panicum virgatum 'Northwind', 301
Papaver atlanticum, 266
    'Flore Pleno', 266
Papaver orientale, 264–266
paper birch, 41
paperbark maple, 73
parking lot, 141, 172, 274
Parthenocissus quinquefolia, 192
    'Star Showers', 192
    'Variegata', 192
Parthenocissus tricuspidata, 180, 191
    'Lowii', 317
partridge feather, 230
Patrinia scabiosifolia, 247
'Peggy Martin' rose, 190
Pennisetum alopecuroides 'Hameln', 290–293
Pennisetum orientale, 292
    'Karley Rose', 278, 292
Pennsylvania sedge, 295
peony, 257–259
Penstemon heterophyllus, 226
    'Blue Springs', 226
    'Electric Blue', 226
    'Margarita BOP', 226
Persicaria affinis, 18, 207
Persicaria amplexicaulis 'Golden Arrow', 216
Persicaria microcephala 'Red Dragon', 200, 216
Persicaria polymorpha, 120

Philadelphus lewisii, 53
    'Cheyenne', 53
Philadelphus ×virginalis 'Miniature Snowflake', 167
phlox, 260–263
Phlox paniculata, 260–263
Phyllostachys, 280–282
Physocarpus opulifolius, 105
    'Coppertina', 105
    'Dart's Gold', 105
    'Diabolo', 105
    'Summer Wine', 1015
Picea bicolor 'Howell's Dwarf Tigertail', 143
Picea pungens, 46–48
pieris, 150–153
Pieris japonica, 150–153
pineapple guava, 93
Pinus mugo, 141
    'Mops', 141
    var. *mugo*, 141
    'Teeny', 141
Pittosporum tenuifolium, 156
    'Golf Ball', 156
    'Silver Sheen', 156
Plains prickly pear, 268
plant names, 29–30
Platanus ×acerifolia, 43
Platanus occidentalis, 43
Platanus orientalis, 43
'Platt's Black' brass buttons, 304
plum yew, 178
plumbago, 236
Poa pratensis, 294–296
Podranea ricasoliana, 187
Podocarpus, 179
    'Icee Blue', 179
Polemonium reptans 'Stairway to Heaven', 235
Polygonatum, 297
    'Variegatum', 297
pomegranate, 163
Poncirus trifoliata, 52
    'Flying Dragon', 133

'Poorinda Royal Mantle'
      grevillea, 299
poppy, 264–266
Populus nigra 'Italica', 78–80
Porteranthus trifoliatus, 209
prairie blazing star, 241
prairie rose, 188
prairie smoke, 205
prickly pear, 258, 267–269
primrose, 270–273
Primula, 270–273
princess flower, 227
privet, 154–156
problem plants, defined, 16–17
prostrate Japanese plum yew, 288
Prunus, 94–96
Prunus laurocerasus 'Otto Luyken', 40
Pueraria lobata, 182
Punica granatum, 163
'Purpurea' acacia, 96
pussy willow, 157–159
Pycnanthemum muticum, 228
pyracantha, 160–163
Pyracantha, 160–163
Pyrus calleryana, 49–51

Q

Quercus macrocarpa, 75
Quercus virginiana, 75–77
quince, 132

R

rabbit brush, 246
rabbiteye blueberry, 114
ragweed, 244
rattlesnake master, 274
ravenna grass, 310
red bird-of-paradise, 86
red mahonia, 129
red maple, 88
redbud, 34, 69
Rhapidophyllum hystrix, 149
rhododendron, 164–166

Rhododendron, 164
Rhododendron, large leaf cultivars,
      164–166
Rhododendron carolinianum, 125
Rhododendron maximum, 164
Rhododendron PJM Group, 125–127
Rhododendron viscosum, 126
Rhus aromatica, 115
   'Gro-Low', 148
Rhus typhina, 148
   'Tiger Eyes', 148
river birch, 98
'Robin Hill' shadblow, 94
'Robyn Gordon' grevillea, 153
rock rose, 169
Rocky Mountain juniper, 102
'Rooguchi' clematis, 186
Rosa, 167–169, 188–190
Rosa 'Ballerina', 189
Rosa Oso Easy series, 168
Rosa 'Peggy Martin', 190
Rosa setigera, 188
Rosa 'The Fairy', 168
Rosa The Knock Out series, 168
rose
      climbing, 188–190
      hybrid tea, 167–169
      low-care shrub, 168
'Rose Carpet' indigo, 313
rose of Sharon, 70
rosebay, 164
rosemary willow, 90
Rosmarinus officinalis 'Prostratus', 289
Rubus pentalobus, 285

S

Sabal minor, 9
Saccharum ravennae, 310
saguaro, 80
Salix alba, 97–99
Salix babylonica, 97–99
Salix caprea, 157–159
Salix discolor, 157–159

Salix elaeagnos, 90
Salix 'Golden Curls', 131
Salix integra 'Hakuro-nishiki', 171
Salix sacchalinensis 'Sekka', 157
Salix 'Scarlet Curls', 131
Sambucus, 72
   'Black Lace', 72
   'Sutherland Gold', 72
Sambucus canadensis, 72
sasanqua camellia, 117
Schizophragma hydrangeoides
      'Moonlight', 193
Sciadopitys verticillata, 64
Scotch broom, 170–172
sea kale, 202
seaberry, 162
sedge, 295
sedum, 13, 263, 303
Sedum, 13, 303
Sedum 'Matrona', 263
Senecio cineraria, 13, 228–230
seven-son flower, 44
shape, in garden design, 21–22
'Shawnee Brave' baldcypress, 66
shopping for plants, 28–29, 30–31
size, in garden design, 22
'Slender Silhouette' sweet gum, 79
snowberry, 135
soil drainage, 25–27
soil fertility, 26–27
soil pH, 26, 28
soil types, 25–26
Solidago, 244–247
Solomon's seal, 297
Sophora secundiflora, 71
Sorghastrum nutans, 309
   'Indian Steel', 309
   'Sioux Blue', 309
Spanish poppy, 266
Spiraea douglasii, 173
Spiraea japonica, 173–175
Spiraea tomentosa, 173
spirea, 173–175

Spodiopogon sibiricus, 300
Stachys byzantina, 13
   'Big Ears', 229
   'Helene von Stein', 23, 229
staghorn sumac, 148
star anise, 41
Stewartia, 116
Stewartia pseudocamellia, 116
Stylophorum diphyllum, 265
sugar maple, 87, 88
summersweet, 123
'Sunburst' St. John's wort, 130
sustainable plants, 9, 17, 20, 294
swamp honeysuckle, 126
sweet bay magnolia, 82
sweet olive, 124
sweetfern, 231
sweetheart rose, 168
Symphoricarpos albus, 135
Symphoricarpos orbiculatus, 135
Symphyotrichum ×dumosus, 220
   'Purple Dome', 220
Symphyotrichum novae-angliae 'Purple
   Dome', 220
Symphyotrichum 'Wood's Pink', 220
Symphyotrichum 'Wood's Purple', 220
Symphytum ×uplandincum 'Axminster
   Gold', 249
Syringa reticulata, 119
Syringa vulgaris, 144–146

T

Tanacetum densum subsp. *amani*, 230
Taxodium distichum 'Shawnee Brave',
   66
Taxus, 176–179
Taxus baccata 'Repandens Aurea', 177
Taxus cuspidata 'Dwarf Bright Gold',
   177
Texas mountain laurel, 71
Texas Ranger, 111, 126
Texas redbud, 69
texture, in garden design, 22

Thermopsis caroliniana, 239
Thuja 'Green Giant', 103
Thuja occidentalis, 65, 67, 102–104
   'Degroot's Spire', 65
Thuja plicata, 103
Thuja standishii, 103
thyme, 296
Thymus, 296
Thymus pulegioides 'Coccineus', 296
Thymus serpyllum, 296
Tiarella cordifolia, 272
Tibouchina heteromalla, 227
Tilia cordata, 49
Trachycarpus fortunei, 147–149
tree cacti, 80
tree cholla, 269
true laurel, 39
Tsuga canadensis, 62–64
tufted hair grass, 291
tupelo, 50

U

Ulmus americana, 59–61
   'Valley Forge', 60
umbrella magnolia, 37

V

Vaccinium angustifolium, 316
Vaccinium ashei, 113
Vaccinium corymbosum, 113
'Valley Forge' elm, 60
variegated aralia, 100
variegated bishop's weed, 283
variegated comfrey, 249
variegated daylily, 222
variegated fleece flower, 216
variegated iris, 251
variegated Jacob's ladder, 235
Verbascum, 240
Verbascum chaixii, 240
Verbascum olympicum, 240
Verbascum 'Southern Charm', 240
Vernonia noveboracensis, 261

Viburnum carlesii, 144
Viburnum lentago, 139
vinca, 312–314
Vinca minor, 312–314
vine maple, 33, 74
Virginia creeper, 192
virgin's bower, 185

W

'Walker's Low' catmint, 255
water needs of plants, 25–27
weeping fig, 136
weeping katsura, 97
weeping willow, 97–99
western red cedar, 103
white cedar, 65, 67
white fir, 46, 319
wine cups, 264
winter hazel, 128
winterberry, 161
wintercreeper, 315–317
wisteria, 197–199
Wisteria frutescens, 198
Wisteria sinensis, 197–199
woolly adelgid, 62

X

Xanthorhiza simplicissima, 283
xeric plants, 127

Y

yarrow, 232
yaupon, 104
yellowroot, 283
yellowwood, 85, 283
yew, 176–179
yucca, 274–277
Yucca filamentosa, 274–277

Z

Zimbabwe creeper, 187

About the Author

Andrew Keys is a writer, designer, consultant, and lifelong gardener, host and producer of *Fine Gardening*'s Garden Confidential podcast, and he blogs at Garden Smackdown. Descended from Mississippi cotton farmers, Andrew was raised with a reverence for the land passed down generations, and first fell in love with plants in the woods of his childhood home. Today, his gardening philosophy centers around our role as stewards of the earth, and he's accredited as an organic land care professional by the Northeast Organic Farming Association. His writing has appeared in *Fine Gardening* and other magazines, he's a member of the Garden Designers Roundtable and Garden Writers Association, and has lectured for the New England Wild Flower Society.